The End of the Second Reconstruction

To my teachers

The End of the Second Reconstruction

Obama, Trump, and the Crisis of Civil Rights

Richard Johnson

polity

The right of Richard Johnson to be identified as Author of this Work has been asserted in accordance with the UK Copyright, Designs and Patents Act 1988.

First published in 2020 by Polity Press

Polity Press
65 Bridge Street
Cambridge CB2 1UR, UK

Polity Press
101 Station Landing
Suite 300
Medford, MA 02155, USA

ISBN-13: 978-1-5095-3833-1
ISBN-13: 978-1-5095-3834-8 (pb)

A catalogue record for this book is available from the British Library.

Library of Congress Cataloging-in-Publication Data

Names: Johnson, Richard, 1991- author.
Title: The end of the second reconstruction : Obama, Trump and the crisis of civil rights / Richard Johnson.
Description: Cambridge, UK ; Medford, MA : Polity, 2020. | Includes bibliographical references and index. | Summary: "Why multi-racial democracy in America is at risk if we don't learn the lessons of history"-- Provided by publisher.
Identifiers: LCCN 2019055871 (print) | LCCN 2019055872 (ebook) | ISBN 9781509538331 (hardback) | ISBN 9781509538348 (paperback) | ISBN 9781509538355 (epub)
Subjects: LCSH: Civil rights--United States. | Democracy--Social aspects--United States. | Obama, Barack--Political and social views. | Trump, Donald, 1946---Political and social views. | United States--Politics and government--2011-2017. | United States--Politics and government--2017-
Classification: LCC JC599.U5 J64 2020 (print) | LCC JC599.U5 (ebook) | DDC 323.0973--dc23
LC record available at https://lccn.loc.gov/2019055871
LC ebook record available at https://lccn.loc.gov/2019055872

Typeset in 11 on 13pt Sabon
by Fakenham Prepress Solutions, Fakenham, Norfolk NR21 8NL
Printed and bound in Great Britain by CPI Group (UK) Ltd, Croydon

For further information on Polity, visit our website:
politybooks.com

Contents

Acknowledgments

This book is both a response to late political developments and a product of a decade of thinking historically about race and American political development. I would like to thank the many academics and friends whom I have met over the past decade or so, living in Cambridge, Oxford, New Haven, and Lancaster. Our conversations about race, class, populism, and political institutions have helped me to think deeply about these topics. Above all, I want to thank those mentors who left the greatest impression during my student years: Nancy Bermeo, Nigel Bowles, Christopher Brooke, Andrew Gamble, Jacob Hacker, Duncan Kelly, Desmond King, Iain McLean, Véronique Mottier, Helen Thompson, and Vesla Weaver. I dedicate this book to them collectively.

This book would not have been possible without the encouragement of my commissioning editor at Polity Press, George Owers. George is not only a great editor, whose input has improved this book, but he is also a very good friend. My life has been much enriched as a consequence of our fortuitous first encounter sitting next to each other at my matriculation dinner at Jesus College, Cambridge. The publication process with Polity has been a delightful experience, and I am very grateful for the feedback from the four anonymous reviewers. Their constructive advice has helped to strengthen this book. I also gladly thank Lee Evans, Tom Kelsey, Desmond King, and Rick Valelly, who read early chapters and gave useful comments.

Finally, thanks must go to my family for their encouragement, especially to my parents, my grandmother, and my uncles Peter, Jeff, and David.

Introduction

[The American] is rarely interested in the past because he is so certain that his future will bear no relation to it ... He assumes that as part of his inheritance that he will have the right continually to go forward.

> Harold Laski, *The American Democracy: A Commentary and Interpretation* (1949: 5)

By any measure, James Meredith had an unusual freshers' week in September 1962. When he walked through the University of Mississippi (Ole Miss) to register for classes, there were fresh bullet holes in the buildings and monuments around him. The smell of tear gas hung in the air. The corridor on the way to the university registrar's office was covered in blood. Two men were dead (Mickey 2015: 4–5, 209–14).

In the weeks to come, when James Meredith went to classes, he sat in barren lecture theaters and under-attended seminar rooms, receiving instruction from lecturers accustomed to much larger audiences. He often dined alone, occasionally dodging stones thrown through the windows as he ate. Students urged each other to ensure that he was "treated as if a piece of furniture of no value ... Let no student speak to him and let his attempt to make friends fall on cold, unfriendly faces." James Meredith was the victim of a "war of ostracism."[1]

Yet, the University of Mississippi's first black student did not lack company. The federal government had seen to that. On the day that James Meredith matriculated, 31,000 federal troops were mobilized in northern Mississippi – more than were stationed at the time on the Korean peninsula (Doyle 2001: 277). Tanks rolled down the university town's plush streets and troops marched through the grounds of Ole Miss. Meredith completed his degree under the watchful eye of three hundred US army troops, garrisoned in Oxford for his protection (Mickey 2015: 213). In living memory, no one had seen anything like it: an American town, occupied by its own government, simply to allow a young black man the opportunity to exercise his equal rights as an American citizen.

Of course, the South had seen such scenes before – but just out of grasp of living memory, if not the collective cultural memory of the region. Under the Military Reconstruction Acts of 1867 and the Enforcement Act of 1870, the federal government sent soldiers to Mississippi and other southern states to guarantee the basic citizenship rights of African Americans. Union general Ulysses Grant made his headquarters in Oxford in 1863 as he prepared the Siege of Vicksburg; ninety-nine years later, President John Kennedy used a desk belonging to Grant to sign the orders to occupy Oxford once again (King and Lieberman 2019). The comparison was not lost on southern commentators. The *Hattiesburg American* lamented after Meredith's successful enrolment, "these indeed are the darkest days for Mississippi since the Civil War and reconstruction. The state has been invaded by federal troops."[2]

Since the withdrawal of federal government troops from the South in the 1870s, Mississippi and every southern state had been under single-party rule. The white supremacist Democrats who governed the state were apoplectic at the idea that – after nearly a century of absence – the federal government had returned to revive multiracial democracy.

Governor Ross Barnett sputtered on television two weeks before Meredith's arrival: "There is no case in history where the Caucasian race has survived social integration ... We will not drink from the cup of genocide." Within hours, an effigy of James Meredith was found hanging from a lamppost outside the student union building, holding a sign that read: "Hail Barnett ... We are proud that our governor stands for constitutional sovereignty."[3]

* * *

There are two mistakes commonly made about democracy in the United States. The first is the belief that the United States is one of the oldest democracies in the world. It is often said that, by the 1830s, the "Jacksonian Era," the United States had become a "mass democracy." In the 1840 presidential election, the two main parties, the Whigs and the Democrats, tried to outdo each other in appeals to the "common man." The Democrats adopted the slogan, "Shall the banks or the people rule?," and the victorious Whigs held mass rallies with working-class symbols of cider and log cabins on banners. With the election of William Henry Harrison, newspapers exulted the "making of a poor man President of the United States" (Cheathem 2018).

Yet, this image of the United States as a longstanding democracy is astonishingly incomplete. It is only accurate insofar as "democracy in America" is understood in white terms. Working-class white men have had the right to vote since the early nineteenth century, but non-whites of all classes won the effective right to vote only half a century ago. The intensity of racial divisions in the United States is the most dramatic form of American exceptionalism. It is impossible to understand democracy and its limits without understanding America's history of racial exclusion, racist governance, and racialized citizenship.

In his classic 1944 study *An American Dilemma*, Gunnar Myrdal argued that the United States was fundamentally a liberal, democratic polity, albeit one plagued by occasional racial prejudices. He argued that all Americans were united by a common creedal commitment to "the essential dignity of the individual human being, of the fundamental equality of all men, and of certain inalienable rights to freedom, justice, and a fair opportunity" (1944: 4). Myrdal acknowledged that there were some failings due to racial prejudice, but "this American Creed is the cement in the structure of this great and disparate nation" (1944: 3). Yet, Myrdal's belief in the fundamentally democratic nature of America's political structure does not stand up to scrutiny. The essential features of a liberal, democratic polity – free and fair elections, multi-party competition, universal franchise, free assembly and speech – were not available to millions of Americans until the mid-twentieth century.

People of Asian birth were not permitted to apply for US citizenship until 1952. The secret ballot was not introduced in Georgia or South Carolina until the 1950s. Until the 1960s, states prohibited public sector workers from joining black civic organizations such as the NAACP (National Association for the Advancement of Colored People). Municipalities passed ordinances barring residents from assembling to promote civil rights or voter registration. Before the mid-1960s, millions of African Americans were unable to vote or run for office because of state constitutions designed to deprive them of their citizenship rights. It was not until the 1970s that all Native Americans could exercise the right to vote (King 2000: 238; Bernd 1972; Mickey 2015: 149, 226; Wade 1998: 331).[4]

The civil rights revolution of the 1950s and 1960s, then, must be understood as a process of democratization. It was a period of what Desmond King (2017) has called "forceful federalism," when all branches of the federal government used their fullest powers to broaden citizenship and democratic inclusion. The civil rights revolution was characterized by a combination of coercive executive intervention (e.g., sending the military to desegregate schools), judicially imposed national standard setting (e.g., overturning state-level bans on interracial marriage, applying a "one person, one vote" standard to all state legislatures), constitutional amendments

(Twenty-Third and Twenty-Fourth Amendments),[5] and rights-affirming congressional legislation (e.g., the Civil Rights Acts of 1957, 1960, and 1964; the Voting Rights Act of 1965, the Fair Housing Act of 1968) on behalf of America's hitherto excluded non-white citizens.

For these reasons, it is impossible to describe the United States as having been a full democracy for much more than five decades. This fact should be basic to every American's understanding of their country's development. Many (white) Americans prefer to imagine their country as one of the world's oldest democracies, but, in fact, it joined the club only relatively recently.

A second mistake is the tendency to portray democratization in the United States as a linear progression of expanding rights toward a "more perfect Union." It is superficially easy to see American political development in terms of a "steady march" of freedom, with America's racial evils – slavery, segregation, material racial inequality – being gradually, but steadily, overcome with each successive generation (Klinkner and Smith 1999). It is tempting to draw a line from the Declaration of Independence to Abraham Lincoln's Gettysburg Address to Martin Luther King's "I Have a Dream" speech to Barack Obama's presidential victory, charting astonishing progress along the way. But to do so would be to ignore the evidence of democratic backsliding throughout US history.

The civil rights revolution of the 1950s and 1960s was not the only episode of the federal government's forceful commitment to multiracial democratization. One hundred years earlier, in the 1860s and 1870s, the federal government, often through little less than military occupation, guaranteed the political rights of African American men. This period, known as Reconstruction, followed the American Civil War of 1861–5. It was marked by high levels of black representation, legislation that expanded access to public services, housing, and education, and the flourishing of black trade unions, civic and fraternal groups, newspapers, and grassroots political organizations.

During Reconstruction, roughly two thousand African Americans were elected to public office and 15 percent of all officeholders in the South were black; twenty African Americans were elected to the US House of Representatives, and two were appointed to the US Senate. In the South Carolina legislature, African American representatives were a majority, the only time in US history this has occurred. For thirty-five days, the child of a slave served as the acting governor of Louisiana. African Americans served on juries and as police officers. They were elected to myriad local and state offices: city councilors, sheriffs, recorders of deeds, prosecuting attorneys, justices of the peace, state superintendents of education, and mayors. At least two black women were appointed to public office.[6] Overall, half of these black elected officials had been slaves, and about 20 percent of them were illiterate (Foner 1993; Tate 2003).

Yet, these numbers were not maintained. By the beginning of the twentieth century, virtually all the black elected officials had been driven from office and black voter registration shrunk by as much as 90 percent. Forceful federalism had ended, and African Americans were left abandoned by the federal government. As a result, the gains won during Reconstruction, including the expansion of education and primitive welfare benefits, were lost. Mass incarceration, mob violence, and labor market exclusion took their place.

In the mid-twentieth century, historians recognized the parallels between the two periods of forceful federalism. In a 1957 article, the historian C. Vann Woodward predicted that the "present struggle for Negro rights ... might even be called the Second Reconstruction" (1957: 240). Both Reconstructions saw rapid advancements in black political power, made possible by the federal government's coordinated commitment to guaranteeing the citizenship rights of all Americans, regardless of race.

A key difference was that Americans expected the Second Reconstruction to endure in a way in which the First Reconstruction did not. In the 1966 edition of his seminal book *The Strange Career of Jim Crow*, Woodward confidently observed that "the Second Reconstruction shows no signs of having yet run its course or even of having slackened its pace" (1966: 8). The First Reconstruction came to an end by 1901 when the last African American was ejected from Congress and state legislatures implemented new, racist constitutions. Congress today retains large numbers of African Americans, and the country even elected a black president, unimaginable in the nineteenth century.

The Obama presidency ought to have been the apogee of the Second Reconstruction, but in many respects it represented its denouement (Harris 2012). One of the bitterest ironies of the Obama presidency was that the election and re-election of the first African American president coincided with the most serious federal judicial challenge to African American voting rights in more than a century. The Supreme Court seriously weakened one of the major legislative tools of the Second Reconstruction, the Voting Rights Act. In *Shelby County v. Holder* (2013) the court ended federal preclearance over local election practices, a crucial guarantee of minority voting rights. The lack of interest by Republicans in Congress and in the White House to overturn this devastating ruling demonstrates the end of a hitherto bipartisan consensus for the civil rights infrastructure of the Second Reconstruction. It had been this bipartisan consensus that caused many to believe that the Second Reconstruction would endure in a way in which the First Reconstruction could not.

Instead, the United States has entered a period of racially polarized partisanship, where partisan and racial preferences increasingly align. It is in the interests of one party (the Republican Party) to raise barriers to minorities' access to voting, while it is essential for the other (the Democratic Party) to reduce such barriers. As with other periods in American history, including the First Reconstruction, democratic state-building (and its reversal) is tied to party-building (Orren and Skowronek 2004; King and Lieberman 2009). In *The Strange Career of Jim Crow*, Woodward claimed that "the Second Reconstruction, unlike the old, was not the monopoly of one of the great political parties" (1966: 9). His assessment is no longer valid.

This book argues that we have witnessed the end of federal commitment to the Second Reconstruction. Both Reconstructions were characterized by the profound expansion of coercive intervention of the American state on behalf of racial minorities, followed by a combination of inactive enforcement and active sabotage. Both Reconstructions were actively deconstructed by the federal judiciary in the midst of seemingly ascendant black elected representation. *The Slaughterhouse Cases* in 1873 (see Chapter 2) and *Shelby County* in 2013 (see Chapter 4) crippled federal civil rights statutes, yet they came when African Americans had historically high levels of descriptive representation in state and federal legislatures. The end of judicial enforcement was followed by change at the presidential level (1876 and 2016) in elections where the new president lacked plurality support in the popular vote, but secured his position through a malapportioned electoral college. Prior partisan change in Congress (1874 and 2010) spelled the end of legislative support for Reconstruction, leaving only constitutional amendments that went unenforced.

The end of the Second Reconstruction has profound implications for the vitality of democracy in the United States. As the collapse of the First Reconstruction indicated, democratic development in the United States is not characterized by a forward march of progress. Rather, it has been marked by periods of rapid expansion, followed by decline. This decline is not irreversible, but it becomes more difficult to overcome as political institutions are inhabited by actors who show no commitment to reconstructing genuine, multiracial democracy in the United States.

Organization of This Book

This book holds that the fate of the First Reconstruction can shed light on the collapse of the Second Reconstruction. This is not the first book to draw systematic comparisons between the two Reconstructions. In *The Two Reconstructions,* Richard Valelly made a major contribution in this respect, but events have shifted in important ways since that book was published in 2004. Crucially, Valelly took for granted that the Second Reconstruction was a success. He began his book with a puzzle: "The historical and social science riddle lies in the contrast between these two reconstructions ... Why did the first effort fail? Why has the second succeeded?" (2004: ix). This book starts from a different premise. It argues that federal commitment to the Second Reconstruction has ended and that its legacy is unravelling. Democratization in the United States is once more characterized by backsliding rather than by persistent and durable advance.

The book, therefore, will outline the rise and fall of the First Reconstruction before moving on to examine the trajectory of the Second. I pay close attention to a period unexamined in Valelly's text: the Obama and Trump presidencies. I hold that there is more continuity in explaining these seemingly very different men's elections than is generally understood. Both men were beneficiaries of finely balanced but sharply racially divided electorates. This rise in racially polarized partisanship was toxic for the First Reconstruction and has poisoned the Second Reconstruction.

Chapter 1 ("The Rise of the First Reconstruction") outlines the inclusion of African Americans in US politics in the nineteenth century. This was the United States' first experiment in multiracial democracy. While many commentators argue that Reconstruction lasted for just over a decade (1865–77), I contend that multiracial democracy endured in some states and localities through grassroots resistance to white supremacy for a further twenty-five years. Reconstruction was not merely a moment of elite representation for African Americans; it was also a period of great popular participation for ordinary African Americans. Union Leagues, local Republican Party branches, school boards, lodges, workers' associations, and churches were all sites of popular black political involvement. Well over a million black agricultural laborers were unionized. In some southern states, a majority of trade union members were black (DeSantis 2016).

Chapter 2 ("The Fall of the First Reconstruction") explains why by the start of the twentieth century all these democratic gains had been reversed. There are myriad explanations for the failure of Reconstruction. Some Marxist historians blame the absence of land reform and the failure to redistribute wealth from white elites to former slaves (Taylor 2008). Some commentators point to black cooptation by white powerbrokers, with black elites delivering a (shrinking) share of the African American vote to white candidates in exchange for access to a limited set of patronage appointments (Reed 2002: 111). Older commentaries proposed that politics advanced too quickly ahead of social attitudes on race (Myrdal 1944), while less generous accounts blamed black incompetence and misrule (Coulter 1947).

I argue in this chapter that the fundamental flaw of the First Reconstruction was the failure of reformers to dismantle the dangerous undemocratic institutions embedded in the US Constitution. Most importantly, the power of the Supreme Court went unchallenged, leaving civil rights reforms vulnerable to judicial attack. The political will to resist this judicial onslaught was lacking as a result of high levels of partisan polarization over civil rights. Only one party – the Republicans – was committed to black enfranchisement and political power. Democrats had every incentive to diminish black voters' access to the polls and to indulge white prejudices about African Americans. When Republicans lost their nerve on the continued deployment of forceful federalism, Democrats reacted, sometimes with the support of violent paramilitaries, to assert political power on racial lines. Democratization is not sustainable if only one party is committed to it.

Chapter 3 ("The Rise of the Second Reconstruction") charts America's second period of democratic expansion in the mid-twentieth century. Minority officeholding, the right to vote, and access to basic public services were all dependent on the massive intervention of the federal government, secured through legislative reforms, judicial rulings, constitutional amendments, and the physical presence of federal agents monitoring the citizenship rights of African Americans. As the example given above of James Meredith shows, multi-racial inclusion was only possible through profound coercive involvement from the federal government.

This chapter will focus, in particular, on the Voting Rights Act of 1965, the most important piece of civil rights legislation ever enacted. As black voter registration and officeholding skyrocketed in the years after its passage, this legislation was said to have produced little less than a "quiet revolution" in voting rights for racial minorities (McDonald 1989; Davidson and Grofman 1994). Its measures, such as the dispatching of federal agents to promote registration and strict federal preclearance rules, demonstrated serious federal commitment to the enforcement of voting rights for African Americans and other minorities. When President Lyndon Johnson signed the bill into law on August 6, 1965, he called the legislation "a triumph for freedom as huge as any victory that has ever been won on any battlefield." At his last press conference as president, Johnson stated that he regarded the Voting Rights Act to be his greatest achievement.

Chapter 4's title ("The Compromise of 2016") is an allusion to the Compromise of 1877, which spelled the end of the forceful federalism that sustained the First Reconstruction. In the 1876 election, as a result of the malapportioned electoral college, it was the loser of the popular vote, Rutherford Hayes, who was awarded the presidency. Hayes's tenure brought executive branch federal support for Reconstruction to an end, coinciding with the loss of Congress by pro-Reconstruction candidates in the previous midterm elections. While elements of the First Reconstruction persisted in fits and starts in varying states and localities, its legacy had, within a generation, been entirely erased. Federal commitment to the Second Reconstruction came to a firm close by 2016, as a result of the sharp increase in racially polarized partisanship and judicial backsliding on civil rights.

The increase in racially polarized partisanship contributed to substantial Democratic losses in Congress and in state legislatures. Barack Obama and Donald Trump were both beneficiaries of extremely racially divided, but finely balanced, electorates. The historically high levels of support and turnout from non-white voters that Obama received in 2008 and 2012 ensured his presidency, but they masked a long-term (and intensifying) decline in white support for the Democrats, which proved devastating for Obama's party in the midterm elections, in state legislatures, and, ultimately, in the election of his successor.

Additionally, this period has seen trenchant judicial challenge to the civil rights infrastructure that had sustained the Second Reconstruction. In particular, in 2013 the Supreme Court in *Shelby County v. Holder* rendered the most powerful element of the Voting Rights Act of 1965 (Section 5) inoperable. The decision was the first since the nineteenth century in which the Supreme Court struck down a major piece of federal civil rights legislation outright. It led to discernible changes in electoral law and practice in areas previously covered by Section 5 of the Act. The weakening of the Voting Rights Act represented not only a setback for minority voting rights, but also a major reversal of American democratization more broadly.

Chapter 5 ("Reconstructing Reconstruction") is a reflection on how best to rescue the Second Reconstruction from failure. The path that followed the failure of the First Reconstruction is not preordained, but Americans must not be so complacent as to believe that democratic backsliding is simply historical artifact. Relatedly, commentators must avoid lazy prognostications that declare "demography is destiny," pointing to the increased proportion of non-whites in the American public as salvation. A majority, non-white electorate is decades away. Additionally, non-white growth in the American population is driven almost entirely by Hispanic and Asian Americans and their children with white partners, whose alignment with the interests of African Americans cannot be assumed.

The US Constitution makes sustained democratization challenging. The institutional structures of American federalism provide areas with less diverse populations a greater say in the American policymaking process. The Constitution affords each state two votes in the Senate, regardless of population differences, which in turn is a basis of the electoral college. The consequence is that states with the most power in deciding crucial national-level policy through the Senate and in electing the president are those that lack the large, diverse populations found in big cities. Constitutional change is itself extremely difficult, due to the Constitution's own amendment procedures. An amendment must command the support of two-thirds of both chambers of Congress and three-quarters of states, giving disproportionate influence to states with lower populations, which are disproportionately white and rural.

The challenge, then, for reconstructing Reconstruction must involve a grassroots, multiracial coalition committed to restoring America's crucial civil rights infrastructure. This coalition can be united by a commitment not only to civil rights, but also to the delivery of general demands for greater equality and economic justice. This "dual agenda" approach was posited by the race theorists Dona and Charles Hamilton (1998), but it has lately been neglected as political actors and commentators have increasingly accepted racially polarized partisanship as a tragic inevitability. I argue in Chapter 5 that the alternative is a form of working-class, multiracial populism.

The book finishes with a reflection on the fragility of democracy in the United States. It overturns linear assumptions about the steady construction of a "more perfect Union." Democratic reversal in the United States is unlikely to take the form of a declaration of martial law or the imposition of single-party rule. Instead, reversal is likely to resemble the processes of the American state itself – with changes that are diffuse and incremental, but which collectively can be hugely consequential. When race and party so closely align, efforts to rewrite the rules of the political game to advantage a particular party inescapably also rewrite the rules to advantage a particular race. Steps that appear individually to be minor, color-blind, or innocuous have the aggregate effect of tilting the playing field away from historically marginalized groups, reasserting historic imbalances in racial power.

1

The Rise of the First Reconstruction

I admit that this species of legislation is absolutely revolutionary. But are we not in the midst of a revolution?
Senator Lot Morrill (R-ME) on the Civil Rights Act of 1866

Abraham Lincoln's support for black suffrage may have cost him his life. On the evening of Tuesday, April 11, 1865, a crowd gathered outside the White House to hear the recently re-inaugurated president speak on the week's momentous events. Two days earlier, General Robert E. Lee had surrendered his Confederate forces to Union general Ulysses S. Grant. Lincoln addressed the "silent, intent, and perhaps surprised multitude" from the window overlooking the building's north door (Brooks 1895: 255). With his 12-year-old son Tad by his side, Lincoln commented, with some buoyancy, on the implications of Lee's surrender for the years to come. The war-weary president spoke of his "gladness in heart" and a "joyous expression that cannot be restrained."

Rather than dwell on the Union's military victory, Lincoln addressed the need for "the re-inauguration of the national authority – reconstruction." He made clear that the Civil

War had readjusted the American constitutional settlement. Two months earlier, Congress had given its overwhelming support to a new amendment to the US Constitution outlawing slavery in every state and federal territory. This amendment extended and reinforced the unilateral action that Lincoln had taken two years earlier to abolish slavery in every state that had taken up arms against the federal government, turning the Civil War from a struggle to preserve the Union to a war of liberation.[1] For Lincoln, the abolition of slavery was, at last, to "be unquestioned and unquestionable."

Lincoln's anti-slavery views were well known and unsurprising. But, in an unexpected move, Lincoln gave a clear steer as to the next phase of postwar reconstruction: he proposed that it was time for black men to be given the right to vote. This was the first time that Lincoln – or, indeed, any US president – had expressed public support for black enfranchisement. In a characteristic spirit of conciliation, which the more radical members of the president's party found deeply frustrating, Lincoln accepted that the black franchise might initially need to be limited to black veterans and those who could read. Lincoln's pronouncement that evening was, nonetheless, a dramatic step. In his eyes, black sacrifice during the Civil War, as well as the sacrifice of others in the Union cause, had made African Americans eligible for US citizenship. This was a significant turnaround for a man who only a decade before had supported the idea of deporting freed slaves to Africa.

Lincoln's first speech in favor of black suffrage was also his last. Unbeknownst to the president, a semi-famous stage actor with southern sympathies was in the crowd on the White House lawn that evening. Hearing the president's multiracial pledge, John Wilkes Booth recoiled: "That means nigger citizenship. Now, by God, I will put him through." Booth vowed: "This will be the last speech he will ever make" (Rhodehamel and Taper 1997: 15). Three days later, on Good Friday, President Lincoln and First Lady Mary Todd Lincoln went to Ford's Theatre in Washington to watch the trans-Atlantic comedy *Our American Cousin*. It was a welcome diversion after four years of misery and war. Lincoln extended an invitation to the triumphant General Grant and his wife Julia to join them in the presidential box. With untold consequences for the future of American politics, Julia Grant persuaded her husband to make their excuses because she loathed the famously temperamental First Lady. Booth had a post-box in the theater and, while collecting his mail earlier in the week, had been tipped off that the president would be attending. Booth knew the script by heart, and at the funniest line in the play, when the president was laughing uproariously, Booth shot him in the back of the head.

The murder of Abraham Lincoln was initially a grave set-back for the cause of Reconstruction. Lincoln's successor Andrew Johnson was not even a Republican. The southern Democrat had been placed on the national ticket with Lincoln during the wartime 1864 election as a gesture to national unity. Lincoln's first vice-president, Hannibal Hamlin, was an ally of the radical, pro-civil rights faction of the Republican Party. Johnson's presence on the ticket was thought to be less divisive.

Johnson had not been chosen to play this role of national healer because he had particularly distinguished himself in public life. There simply weren't many options. He was the only southern senator who remained loyal to the Union during the Civil War. A warrior for the white working class from which he emerged, Johnson hated the slave-owning aristocracy so much that he refused to endorse their Confederate project.

Hating the slaveholding elite and even being opposed to slavery did not necessarily mean support for black civil rights. As Desmond King and Rogers Smith (2005) have pointed out, many opponents of slavery were also white supremacists. The Oregon Territory exhibited this powerfully in 1857. On the same day that 74.5 percent of Oregonians voted to ban slavery in the territory, 88.9 percent voted to make it illegal for African Americans to live in Oregon at all.

A Unionist out of spite and class hatred, Johnson was vulgar, self-obsessed, and a drunk. He was "intolerant to criticism" and paranoid about his political opponents. As president, he believed them to be plotting his impeachment (justifiably) and his assassination (fantasy). He was also deeply self-absorbed. In a speech intended to mark the birthday of George Washington, he mentioned himself more than two hundred times in sixty minutes (Foner 1988).

Johnson confirmed everyone's low expectations at the ceremony for his vice-presidential inauguration on March 4, 1865. Before giving his speech, he asked his predecessor Hannibal Hamlin to fetch him a bottle of whiskey. Hamlin, a teetotaler, had banned the sale of alcohol on Capitol Hill, but a special accommodation was made for the new vice-president. Suitably imbibed, Johnson proceeded to give a rambling speech, while Abraham Lincoln and the nation's dignitaries looked on in horror:

> I'm a-goin' for to tell you here to-day; yes, I'm a-goin' for to tell you all, that I am a plebeian! I glory in it. I am a plebeian! The people yes, the people of the United States have made me what I am; and I am a-goin' for to tell you here to-day yes, today, in this place that the people are everything. We owe all to them. If it be not too presumptuous, I will tell the foreign ministers a-sittin' there that I am one of the people. I will say to senators and others before me. I will say to the Supreme Court, which sits before me that you all get your power and place from the people.

Hannibal Hamlin, aghast, tugged on his successor's coat. "Johnson," he hissed, "stop!" Undeterred, Johnson continued. The new vice-president looked down at the officials assembled in the Senate chamber and began to call them each by name. "And I will say to you Mr. Chase [Chief Justice], your position depends on the people! And I will say to you Mr. Secretary Seward [Secretary of State] ..." When he came to the Secretary of the Navy, memory failed. Leaning over to a Senate official, Johnson asked in a stage whisper,

"What is the name of the Secretary of the Navy?" Informed, Johnson resumed, "And I say to you Mr. Secretary Welles. You all derive your power from the people." Hamlin pulled at Johnson's coat again, begging him to stop. But, Johnson, euphoric and oblivious, blethered on (Browne 2008: 197–8; Stewart 2009: 8–9).

For those who hoped that the somber circumstances under which Johnson assumed the presidency might have transformed him, they were soon disappointed.[2] A month after Lincoln's murder, President Johnson hosted the "Grand Review of the Armies" in which more than 80,000 victorious Union troops paraded through Washington, DC to celebrate the end of the Civil War. As a sign of things to come, however, the United States Colored Troops (the Union's all-black regiments) were excluded from the parade. They had composed about one-tenth of the Union's forces.

The African Americans who marched in the Grand Review were captured slaves from General Sherman's march, who, in spite of having been emancipated from slavery, were dressed in colorful outfits like clowns for comical effect. Taller African American men were made to sit on little donkeys that were much too small, with their feet dragging on the ground. From the reviewing stand in front of the White House, President Johnson and other dignitaries laughed "heartily" at the sight (McConnell 1992).

* * *

This chapter charts the rise of the First Reconstruction. It argues that major legislative and constitutional reforms enacted by Congress and eventually enforced by a supportive presidential administration democratized the United States. The reforms resulted in the election and appointment of nearly two thousand black men and even some black women to public office in the second half of the nineteenth century. This chapter shows that these top-level reforms were complemented by vibrant black grassroots activism, with black civic organizations, fraternal clubs, local party organizations, and trade unions providing the lifeblood for a lively multiracial democracy, which was the first of its kind in the world.

Democratizing the Constitution

In his first months as president, Andrew Johnson appeared to be a disaster for the cause of Reconstruction. He pardoned Confederate soldiers, installed white supremacists as governors in the southern states, and vetoed funding for the Freedmen's Bureau. Southern states, with the president's backing, implemented "black codes," which were designed to return African Americans as close to the position of slavery as possible. Vague crimes such as "vagrancy" (effectively, unemployment) were used to arrest African Americans who were not seen as sufficiently industrious or subservient. Some of these crimes could carry life sentences, leading to a life of involuntary servitude, in spite of the abolition of slavery. In Alabama, for instance, the white supremacist governor Lewis Parsons, a Johnson appointee, stipulated that a sheriff could imprison anyone who did not prove that they were employed, and then the prisons could contract their labor to defray the costs of incarceration (McCrary 1984).

Johnson's powers, however, were not unlimited. Shortly before Lincoln died, the Republican Party won huge majorities in Congress (see Figure 1.1). In the House, 76 percent of districts were in Republican hands, and 81 percent of senators were Republicans. This placed the Republican Congress in a powerful position. The US Constitution gives Congress the authority to rule without the president's agreement if there is sufficient political will to do so. Unlike in some political systems, if the legislative branch can muster two-thirds support, then executive consent is not necessary for legislation. Constitutional amendments do not require the president's signature at all.

Additionally, the Constitution ensures that impeachment is a political, not purely legal, process. There is no "burden of proof" that Congress must legally meet to remove a president for "high crimes and misdemeanors." Incensed by

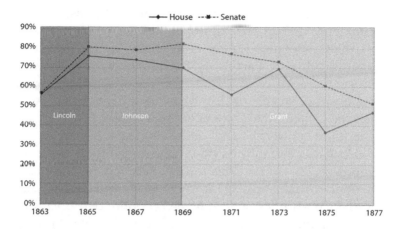

Figure 1.1: Republican strength in Congress during federal Reconstruction (1863–77)
Source: My own creation; data taken from: "Party Divisions of the House of Representatives, 1789 to Present" (https://history.house.gov/Institution/Party-Divisions/Party-Divisions/) and "Party Division" (https://www.senate.gov/history/partydiv.htm)

the president's behavior and opposition to civil rights, 73 percent of members of the US House of Representatives voted to impeach Johnson. Among the articles of impeachment were included incriminations about his "utterances, declarations, threats, and harangues," which were "peculiarly indecent and unbecoming in the Chief Magistrate of the United States." Johnson had "brought [the] high office of the President of the United States into contempt, ridicule, and disgrace, to the great scandal of all good citizens." The House decided that these actions alone constituted "a high misdemeanor." On May 26, 1868, considering these and other charges, 64.8 percent of senators voted to remove Johnson from office – one vote short of the two-thirds threshold. The one vote, which saved Johnson's presidency, was cast by Senator David Patterson, his son-in-law.

In spite of their narrow failure to remove Johnson from office and replace him with the radical Senate president pro tempore Benjamin Wade, the Republican Party was able to pass sweeping civil rights legislation and constitutional amendments during the anti-civil rights president's term. With their moderate leader Lincoln dead, the leadership of the Republican Party fell to its senior congressional spokesmen, who came from the party's radical wing. Republicans pursued a project of democratization the like of which the United States had never seen before.

The most powerful and enduring legal legacy of the Reconstruction period consisted of the three "Reconstruction amendments" to the US Constitution. Between the ratification of the Bill of Rights in 1791 and the Civil War seventy years later, the Constitution was amended on only two occasions. Both amendments were technical clarifications: foreign governments could not sue the US government in federal court (Eleventh Amendment, 1795) and members of the electoral college needed to cast separate ballots for the president and the vice-president (Twelfth Amendment, 1803). The Civil War, in contrast, produced three new amendments within five years, which fundamentally changed property relations, the balance of power in the state–federal relationship, and the meaning of and eligibility for US citizenship. The Thirteenth Amendment abolished slavery in 1865. The Fourteenth Amendment, ratified in 1868, addressed the citizenship rights of the ex-slaves. In 1870, the Fifteenth Amendment explicitly forbade racial discrimination in voting.

The Thirteenth Amendment to the US Constitution was the most far-reaching confiscation of private wealth in Western history outside communism. While the British Empire used taxpayer money to compensate slaveholders when Parliament abolished slavery in 1833, American slaveholders received no such financial assistance. Efforts to claim compensation were made by southern whites after the Civil War, but they were rebuffed (Kleintop 2018). It is important to understand that the "value" of southern slaves represented a greater share of American gross domestic product than all of northern industry combined.[3] The cost of emancipation, if compensated, would have been $2.7 billion in an economy with a GDP of $4.2 billion (Goldin 1974: 73–4).

The Thirteenth Amendment is the only addition to the US Constitution that explicitly protects labor rights (Zackin 2013). American liberals have been reluctant to take seriously the materialist implications of the amendment.[4] It was not only an expansion of political rights, but its non-compensatory content was an attack on property-oriented liberalism, which had shamefully been making excuses for slaveholding since the writings of John Locke (1632–1704) (Macpherson 1963; Glausser 1990).[5] The richest Americans lived in the Mississippi Delta and South Carolina rice kingdom. These white elites were not simply rich from the crops they sold; they had financialized slaveholding, turning slaves into valuable collateral for loans and sources of credit (Kilbourne 1995; Martin 2010; Rosenthal 2018). Depriving these elites of their wealth was one of the most radical policy outcomes of America's bloodiest ever conflict. The Thirteenth Amendment represented, at long last, the defeat of the powerful slaveholding class. As Keeanga-Yamahtta Taylor (2008) writes, "in one fell swoop, the majority of the southern aristocracy was destroyed – physically, morally, and economically."

The Fourteenth Amendment was really more like four or five constitutional amendments rolled into one. The first three sections provided a constitutional basis for civil rights legislation. They guaranteed citizenship to every person born in the United States; they ensured equal due process; and they guaranteed equal protection under the law for all Americans, regardless of which state they inhabited. Second, the Fourteenth Amendment tipped the balance of power away from state governments toward the federal government by prohibiting any state from restricting the "privileges and immunities" that individuals enjoyed by virtue of US citizenship. This was a complete nationalization of US citizenship and repudiated the idea that Americans had a dual "state citizenship" which might provide them different rights to their national citizenship.

Third, the Fourteenth Amendment provided a constitutional basis for attacking white supremacist political power. It barred former Confederates from holding office. It forbade the federal government from using US taxpayer money to finance Confederate war debt or provide financial compensation for the abolition of slavery. Finally, it implicitly guaranteed black suffrage by empowering Congress with the ability to reduce the congressional representation of any state that failed to provide universal suffrage to all men over the age of twenty-one. Women's suffrage campaigners balked at the specification that limited this guarantee to "any of the male inhabitants" only.

The Fifteenth Amendment codified an end to racial discrimination in voting, which had already been implicit in the Fourteenth Amendment's guarantee to equal citizenship. With Republicans' two-thirds majority in the House slipping away, President Ulysses Grant – who had taken over the presidency in 1869 – liberally used his patronage powers to ensure that the amendment found the required support in Congress. Once ratified, the elated president broke with custom and affixed a personal letter to Congress lauding the amendment. It was a symbolic signature of approval that he was not constitutionally required to provide. Grant celebrated the "measure which makes at once 4,000,000 people voters who were heretofore declared by the highest tribunal in the land not citizens of the United States, nor eligible to become so." He reflected that it was "a measure of grander importance than any other one act of the kind from the foundation of our free government to the present day."

These democratizing amendments were accompanied by about half a dozen federal statutes, which sought to guarantee the full fruits of citizenship to black men (see Table 1.1), starting with the Freedman's Bureau Act, passed one month before Lincoln's death, and ending with the Civil Rights Act of 1875, passed in the lame-duck session after Grant lost his majority in the House of Representatives.

The Freedmen's Bureau Act provided social services to African Americans. The Bureau was tasked with establishing schools for ex-slaves, as well as providing them with emergency food, shelter, and healthcare. For example, after a flood in the Red River Valley of Louisiana in 1866, the Bureau seized some planters' cotton, cashed it out, and distributed

Table 1.1: The legal infrastructure of the First Reconstruction (1865–75)

Law	Year	Type	President	Content
Freedmen's Bureau Act	1865	Statute	Abraham Lincoln (Approved)	Created the Freedmen's Bureau, provided social services for ex-slaves
Thirteenth Amendment	1865	Constitutional amendment	Abraham Lincoln (N/A)	Abolished slavery
Civil Rights Act of 1866	1866	Statute	Andrew Johnson (Veto – Overridden)	Guaranteed equal civil and political rights
Military Reconstruction Acts	1867	Statute	Andrew Johnson (Veto – Overridden)	Occupied the South, registered voters, required new state constitutions
Fourteenth Amendment	1868	Constitutional amendment	Andrew Johnson (N/A)	Guaranteed equal citizenship, centralized powers of national government
Fifteenth Amendment	1870	Constitutional amendment	Ulysses Grant (N/A)	Prohibited racial discrimination in voting
Enforcement Act	1870	Statute	Ulysses Grant (Approved)	Sent additional troops to the South, outlawed white supremacist groups
Naturalization Act of 1870	1870	Statute	Ulysses Grant (Approved)	Immigrants of African descent can become naturalized US citizens
Ku Klux Klan Act	1871	Statute	Ulysses Grant (Approved)	Supported legal prosecution of KKK members
Civil Rights Act of 1875	1875	Statute	Ulysses Grant (Approved)	Barred segregation in public spaces and businesses

the benefits to former slaves who had not yet been paid (Lane 2008). The Bureau also arbitrated contracts between ex-slaves and plantation owners, ensuring that former masters did not exploit their formerly unpaid laborers. After Lincoln's assassination, Andrew Johnson vetoed a bill to provide extra funding to the Freedmen's Bureau, claiming it was totally irresponsible given "the condition of our fiscal affairs." Astonishingly, in the same message, Johnson told Congress that he was better placed to speak for the general welfare of the country because he had been "chosen by the people of all the States" rather than "from a single district." A member of Congress retorted sarcastically that Johnson "is modest for a man ... made president by an assassin" (Foner 1988).

Congress needed two-thirds of its strength to legislate without Johnson's approval. Determined to push forward with their vision of Reconstruction, Congress overrode Johnson's veto of the Civil Rights Act of 1866, the first piece of comprehensive civil rights legislation in US history. The Civil Rights Act granted citizenship to African Americans, guaranteed their civil rights, and strengthened the Freedmen's Bureau. In 1867, Congress once more disregarded Johnson by passing the Military Reconstruction Acts, which sent 20,000 federal troops to occupy the South to protect black civil and voting rights. US soldiers were tasked with actively registering African Americans to vote. Within a matter of months, concentrated in the summer of 1867 – called the "registration summer" by Julie Saville (1996: 160) – the proportion of African Americans registered to vote rose from 1 percent of the adult male population to over 80 percent. Eric Foner (1988: 282) calls 1867 an *annus mirabilis*.

The 1868 election, in which Ulysses Grant was elected to become president, changed the hitherto toxic dynamic between the legislative and executive branches. The new Republican administration meant that Congress would now only need a simple majority of its members to pass further civil rights statutes. During the Grant administration, Congress passed the Civil Rights Act of 1870, which created the Department of Justice; the Enforcement Act and the Ku

Klux Klan Act, which targeted white supremacist groups; and the Civil Rights Act of 1875, which prohibited racial discrimination in public services and transport.

Congress also liberalized immigration law, allowing people of African descent to become naturalized US citizens. In 1790, one of the first-ever acts of Congress had restricted eligibility for US citizenship to "free whites" only. The Naturalization Act of 1870 ensured that slaves who had been born in Africa as well as immigrants from Africa and the Caribbean could apply for citizenship. The failure to include Asian Americans was not corrected until 1952, barring Asian-born people from becoming US citizens for another eighty-two years.

The creation of the Department of Justice by the Civil Rights Act of 1870 was one of the most durable administrative legacies of the First Reconstruction. President Grant appointed Amos Akerman to head this new department oriented toward protecting newly freed African Americans' citizenship rights. Akerman had written a staunch letter of support for Grant during the 1868 election and recorded his view that "the abolition of all political distinctions founded on color will remove effectually and forever all danger of conflict between the races."[6] In this spirit, Akerman used his role as attorney general to prosecute Ku Klux Klan members across the South. He wrote in 1871 that "extraordinary means" were needed to suppress the Klan. "These combinations," he warned, "amount to war and cannot be effectually crushed on any other theory" (White 2016: 526). Under Akerman's direction, more than three thousand Klansmen were arrested, with the worst offenders placed on trial before racially integrated juries (Foner 1988: 457–8). Within a few years, the Justice Department, as Robert Kaczorowski puts it, "succeeded in destroying the Klan" (2005: 79). It was the first lesson in the profound role that the Department of Justice could play in the delivery of political power to African Americans.

The radicals in the Republican Party understood that this legal framework amounted to a democratic revolution in the United States. At the outset, Congressman Thaddeus Stevens told his constituents in Lancaster, Pennsylvania:

But it is revolutionary, say they. This plan would, no doubt, work a radical reorganization in Southern institutions, habits, and manners. It is intended to revolutionize their principles and feelings. This may startle feeble minds and shake weak nerves. So do all great improvements in the political and moral world. It requires a heavy impetus to drive forward a sluggish people. When it was first proposed to free the slaves and arm the blacks ... the prim conservatives, the snobs, and the male waiting-maids in Congress, were in hysterics ...

The whole fabric of Southern society must be changed, and never can it be done if this opportunity is lost. Without this, this government can never be, as it never has been, a true republic. Heretofore, it had more the features of aristocracy than of democracy. The Southern States have been despotisms, not governments of the people ... Let us forget all parties, and build on the broad platform of "reconstructing" the government out of the conquered territory converted into new and free States.[7]

Stevens's recognition that America "never has been a true republic" was important. It confirmed that the Civil War was a democratic revolution in a way in which the American War of Independence simply was not. The American Revolution was a victory for the slaveholding class, from which George Washington, Thomas Jefferson, and James Madison hailed. The ethos of the Civil War was of an altogether different character. Senator Lot Morrill, a radical Republican from Maine, exclaimed in the Senate chamber in 1866: "I admit that this species of legislation is absolutely revolutionary. But are we not in the midst of a revolution?" He contended that Reconstruction would constitute America's first democratic revolution. It is hard to disagree.

Executive Branch Enforcement

As would become evident once more during the Second Reconstruction, the radical democratic legal infrastructure erected by Congress would only be effective insofar as the national government was willing to deploy its coercive power to enforce it (Kato 2015; King 2017). Enforcement was achieved by establishing a federal military presence in the South and through the vigorous prosecution of crimes of racial violence. To enable African Americans to be equal citizens, the federal government needed to place parts of the United States under military occupation.

Congress took advantage of the Union victory to compel the defeated South to embrace multiracial democracy. The Military Reconstruction Acts of 1867 were designed to put the Thirteenth Amendment and Civil Rights Act of 1866 into effect. President Johnson unsuccessfully vetoed the legislation, warning it would result in "Africanizing the southern part of our territory" and that "the purpose and object of the bill – the general intent which pervades it from beginning to end – is to change the entire structure and character of the State governments and to compel them by force to the adoption of organic laws and regulations which they are unwilling to accept if left to themselves." Johnson denounced that the legislation would "force the right of suffrage out of the hands of the white people and into the hands of the negroes." He added, disingenuously: "The negroes have not asked for the privilege of voting; the vast majority of them have no idea what it means." In this, he would soon be proven wrong.

As Johnson correctly understood, the three Military Reconstruction Acts shifted legitimate political power away from the forces of white supremacy and to African American citizens and their allies. They did so in four ways.

First, they declared nearly all of the South to be under military control and overthrew the racist civilian governments that Johnson had helped install after Lincoln's death.

Second, Congress required the creation of new civilian governments in the southern states, but the old state constitutions would need to be torn up. New state constitutions were required, and Congress insisted that they be written by state conventions elected on a multiracial franchise. US soldiers occupied areas of the highest racial tension to ensure that this process took place peacefully. Left with few options, some white Democrats boycotted the constitutional conventions and state referendums, hoping to render them inquorate and illegitimate. These tactics were ignored, and the result was to empower Republican forces – blacks and supportive whites – further. In some states, the new constitutions were written by majority black conventions (McMillan 1955: 110–74; McCrary 1984).

Third, Congress temporarily stripped former Confederates of the right to vote, enabling African Americans and sympathetic whites to win political power under the newly written state constitutions.

Finally, the southern states were required to ratify the Fourteenth Amendment as a precondition of re-establishing their representation in Congress. The amendment process usually empowers states at the expense of national majorities. The requirement that constitutional amendments must receive the backing of three-quarters of states is an extremely high barrier. Making congressional representation contingent on ratification was an ingenious way to pass an amendment that fundamentally stripped rights from the states. It is hard to see how such a centralizing amendment could have passed without this creative move.

The ratification of the Fourteenth Amendment was also politically necessary for congressional Republicans. At the Constitutional Convention in 1787, it was decided that slaves – who were legally property – should count for three-fifths of a person for purposes of congressional apportionment. With the abolition of slavery, blacks were counted equally with whites, thus boosting the value of each African American in the South for purposes of congressional representation by 40 percent. In spite of relative population decline of 4.3 percent over the 1860s and the addition of three new states to the North, the end of the three-fifths rule meant that the South lost almost none of its share of seats in the US House of Representatives after the 1870 Census (see Table 1.2).[8] It was imperative that the beneficiaries of the South's representational gains were African American voters, not white supremacists.

Table 1.2: Change in population and congressional representation (1860–70)

	% of US population			% of seats in House of Representatives		
	1860	1870	Change	1860	1870	Change
Southern states	29.2	24.9	–4.3	25.3	25.0	–0.3
Non-southern states	70.8	75.1	+4.3	74.7	75.0	+0.3

While the Military Reconstruction Acts were transformative in many ways, they were not strong enough to guarantee black voting rights in all parts of the South. The military was overstretched, and there were pockets of the South where local anti-democratic actors reigned supreme. As Matthew Christensen (2012: 2) describes it: "Democratic paramilitary organization[s]" were formed "to remove Republican office-holders from their positions." Where the federal military could not be, black lives were under serious threat from political violence.

This was no more tragically apparent than in St. Landry Parish, Louisiana. While federal troops had a robust presence in New Orleans, helping to integrate the city's public services and even schools, St. Landry was in the remote, rural depths of the state. Local African Americans were in a buoyant spirit with the ratification of the new Louisiana state constitution, which guaranteed equality "without regard to race, color, or previous condition of servitude." The local Republican newspaper, *The Progress*, was a vibrant organ of the party. The newspaper offices were situated within a party clubhouse, which attracted 200–400 attendees at its weekly meetings. The *Progress* headquarters held various party documents, including membership records.

These membership records were used to tragic effect by white supremacists, who went on a killing spree of 200–250 black Republican activists in the parish in the lead-up to the 1868 presidential election (Christensen 2012: 42, 62). Even though more than two thousand African Americans had registered with the Republican Party in the parish the year before, on election day in 1868, not a single vote was cast for Republican Ulysses Grant.

The St. Landry massacre was not a lone incident of its kind during Reconstruction. In the small Georgia town of Camilla (population 289), about a dozen black citizens were murdered at a Republican Party rally in the lead-up to the 1868 election (Formwalt 1987). Indeed, throughout the South, wherever federal troops were unable to position themselves due to lack of personnel, white supremacist vigilantes took their place. These Democrats claimed that they were monitoring the elections to ensure there was no "fraud." The secret ballot was not introduced in some southern states until the 1950s; so it was impossible for voters to conceal their preferences from these informal party "guards" (Bernd 1972; Mickey 2015: 149). There could be fatal consequences for any voter who dared to take a Republican ticket.

In the wake of the 1868 election, Congress knew that it needed even more robust measures to protect black citizenship. Ulysses Grant was elected and re-elected in large part due to the support of African Americans. It is probable that, in both elections, Grant owed his popular vote majorities to the black community, and in 1872 his re-election was largely creditable to exceptionally high turnout from African Americans. William Gillette (1979: 40–1) estimates that black turnout exceeded white turnout that year, a feat not again repeated until Barack Obama's re-election in 2012.

Given how important African American voters were becoming for the Republican Party, President Grant's re-election depended on their protection. On February 21, 1870, Grant signed the Enforcement Act, which sent additional troops into the South. In South Carolina, for example, the number of federal troops occupying the state rose from 427 to 1,019 between 1870 and 1871 (Valelly 2004: 95). It is important to keep in context that the United States was running a larger peacetime military than it had ever done before. In the 1850s, the average annual size of the US military was 24,228 troops, while during Reconstruction

(1866–76), the figure was 51,818.[9] Federal troops occupying the South during Reconstruction were disproportionately black. At the end of the war, then-General Grant first mustered out soldiers who had been serving the longest. Because black regiments were not formed until the later stages of the war, black soldiers were overly represented in the troops that remained.

The Enforcement Act of 1870 contained clear provisions against white supremacist violence. Section 5 of the Act outlawed any "attempt to prevent, hinder, control, or intimidate any person from exercising or in exercising the right of suffrage to whom the right of suffrage is secured or guaranteed by the Fifteenth Amendment to the Constitution." It listed unacceptable behavior, including bribes, threats of violence, ejecting a person from their rented property, refusing to renew leases for property, refusing to renew labor contracts, sacking an employee, and others. Section 6 of the Act clearly targeted the Ku Klux Klan by prohibiting two or more people from going "in disguise upon the highway or upon the premise of another with the intent to violate any provision of this act." The act carried a penalty of ten years' imprisonment for such behavior.

The Enforcement Act, however, relied on federal prosecutors, which in effect decentralized enforcement. The Ku Klux Klan Act, passed the following year, gave direct authority to the president to suspend the writ of habeas corpus in areas dominated by Klan violence. Under this law, thousands of Klan members were arrested and tried in a federal court, often in front of majority black juries. The Secret Service, which had initially been established to combat counterfeiting, was redeployed under its chief Hiram Whitley, a Grant appointee, to infiltrate the Klan and send Klan supporters to prison (Lane 2019).

President Andrew Johnson sympathized with white supremacists and made excuses for white supremacist violence. Only weeks after the massacres surrounding the 1868 election, Johnson informed Congress that he believed it was civil rights activists who were to blame, rather than the whites who had murdered them. He lamented, implausibly: "The attempt to place the white population under the domination of persons of color in the South has impaired, if not destroyed, the kindly relations that had previously existed between them."[10]

Grant took a different view. He regarded white supremacists as anti-democratic agents who fundamentally threatened the hard-fought gains of the Civil War and Reconstruction. There was, of course, an electoral incentive for Grant to protect black voting rights (Malone 2008; Polgar 2011), but there was also a deeper sense that the Civil War was a national struggle for democracy. If the democratic gains were eroded, then it besmirched the sacrifice of the Union forces. A *Chicago Tribune* editorial captured this mood: "We tell the white men in Mississippi that the men of the North will convert your state into a frog pond before they will allow [racist] laws to disgrace one foot of soil in which the bones of our soldiers sleep and over which the flag of freedom waves" (Klinkner and Smith 1999: 79). With that vigorous spirit, the Grant administration relentlessly pursued the Ku Klux Klan. Matthew Christensen concluded: "With these new powers, federal agencies were able to successfully destroy structures of Democratic secret societies" (2012: 85). By the end of Grant's presidency, the Ku Klux Klan had been entirely dismantled.

Black Officeholding

National commitment to protecting African Americans' equal citizenship, by military occupation in some cases, had profound – almost unbelievable – implications for black political power. Some two thousand African Americans entered public office during the First Reconstruction: a governor, six lieutenant governors, two US senators, twenty US congressmen, two ambassadors, hundreds of state legislators, mayors, city and county councilors, judges, state superintendents of education, state treasurers, secretaries of state, state commissioners of agriculture, school board members, recorders of deeds, tax collectors, sheriffs, prosecuting attorneys, and more. About half of these officials had been born into slavery, and about one in five were illiterate (Foner 1993). There are even recorded instances of black women appointed to political patronage posts.

At the height of black officeholding during Reconstruction, about one in three southern political officeholders was black. Only a decade earlier, one in three southerners had been a slave. In the 1868–76 period of Reconstruction, when there was a federal military presence in the South, in an average year there were 268 black state legislators serving throughout the region – a number not repeated, even nationwide, until the 1990s (Valelly 2004: Ch 4). David Bateman (2019) is correct to describe Reconstruction as "one of the most radical projects of democratization in world history." Eric Foner, who has done more than anyone else to rescue these pioneering officeholders from historical obscurity or infamy, described the political situation of the South in the 1870s as follows: "The spectacle of former slaves representing the South Carolina rice kingdoms and the Mississippi cotton belt in the state legislatures, assessing taxes on the property of their former owners, and serving on juries alongside them, epitomized the political revolution wrought by Reconstruction" (1993: xii).

States' and cities' power structures were transformed. African Americans formed a majority in the South Carolina House of Representatives – a situation that has never again occurred in any state legislature in the United States. African Americans won control of city government in Washington, DC, and desegregated the city's public services and amenities (Green 1967: Ch 6). Four African Americans became speakers of their state's House of Representatives. On April 29, 1874, a congressman who had been born a slave was handed the Speaker's gavel and symbolically presided over a debate in the US House of Representatives (Frielander and Gerber 2019: 98). To fill the unexpired term of ex-Confederate President Jefferson Davis, the Mississippi state legislature appointed an African American, Hiram Revels, to the US Senate.

This extraordinary expression of elite-level black politics would not have been possible without the massive commitment of hundreds of thousands of ordinary African Americans to secure and exercise their voting rights. The bravery of working-class African Americans cannot go unacknowledged. Histories of Reconstruction are replete with anecdotes of their quiet heroism and defiance. Foner (1987) records black maids and cooks reporting to work in rural Mississippi wearing badges that bore the image of the Republican presidential candidate – and, to southern whites, despised Union general – Ulysses Grant.

Black turnout was astonishingly high. In some elections, it was estimated to be 90 percent of eligible black voters; indeed, as we have seen, blacks often turned out at higher rates than whites (Gillette 1979: 40–1). This level of participation is all the more impressive given the perennial threats of violence (and actual violence) experienced by black activists. To protect themselves, black Americans pursued a variety of strategies. Black Civil War veterans formed ad hoc marching companies to guide fellow African Americans on the way to the polls in areas where there were insufficient numbers of federal troops. African American workers defied economic sanctions to participate in elections. Even though some plantation owners refused to employ farmers who were active in the Republican Party, many African Americans remained loyal to their politics, in spite of harsh economic repercussions (Fitzgerald 1989: 207–11).

A vibrant black political and civic culture emerged not only at election times: it was a sustained effort. Fraternal clubs, tied to the Republican Party, attracted the membership of hundreds of thousands of ordinary African American citizens. They were institutions for refining political skills, cultivating political efficacy, and political socialization. At its peak, there were two thousand chapters of the Union League club, with about 200–300,000 African American members (Gibson and King 2016). Middle-class African Americans joined the Prince Hall Free Masons, an early black business group (Muraskin 1975).

These enormous gains in black political power were strongly resisted, as will be discussed in Chapter 2. One newspaper reflected that white southerners would have preferred "to see the Devil himself in Congress" than an African American.[11] But the federal presence in the South ensured that the minority of white supremacists who resisted black political advancement were kept at bay. Even after the national Republican Party and federal government abandoned them in 1877, African Americans struggled on in their states and localities for another generation, trying to keep the flame of Republican politics alive until they were fully disenfranchised by the start of the twentieth century.

Policy Consequences

The election of African Americans to public office was not simply a triumph of descriptive representation. It also delivered substantive benefits to both African Americans and the poor. At a time when social policy was broadly a matter for the states – with the significant exception of federal veterans' pensions, a precursor to Social Security (Skocpol 1992) – black control of southern state legislatures saw new guarantees for universal state education, the foundation of public institutions of higher education, wage and labor protections, and even limited experiments with land reform and redistribution.

For many black elected officials, education was their first policy priority. At the federal level, one ex-slave argued in favor of federal funding for education. He recalled to his fellow members of Congress in 1872 that "to educate the Negro was to set him free, and that to deprive him of all of the advantages necessary to enable him to acquire an education was to perpetuate his enslavement."[12]

The African American delegates who drafted their states' new constitutions made sure that they contained provisions for state education. Indeed, every new state constitution under the Military Reconstruction Acts guaranteed a universal right to education. By 1877, there were 572,000 black children attending school in the South (Valelly 2004: 82). On top of guarantees to educate their states' children, many state legislatures created publicly funded universities and technical colleges. There were also some attempts at educational integration. In some parts of Louisiana, black and white children briefly attended the same schools, eight decades before *Brown v. Board of Education* declared "separate but equal" to be unconstitutional. The first integrated class of the University of South Carolina graduated in 1874 (Burke 2000).

Integration in the wider public sphere was another priority. Black state legislators passed laws that integrated public transport and public spaces such as parks and cemeteries, as well as the civic sphere (e.g., juries, public meetings). Private businesses that provided "public accommodations," such as hotels and theaters, were required to be integrated in some states. States also passed declarations of natural, civil, and political equality. The Civil Rights Act of 1875 instituted integration as national policy, but it was the black state legislators who paved the way at the state level.

Demonstrating that economic and political liberty went hand-in-hand, the legislatures also passed early labor protections. As soon as slavery ended, white capitalists sought ways to subjugate black workers, with the "black codes" legally limiting their rights in the states. States exploited a loophole in the Thirteenth Amendment, which allowed them to contract out prisoners to work for private businesses without pay. One observer wrote: "It is their hope and intention, under the guise of the vagrant laws, to restore all of slavery but its name" (Stanley 1998: 126). Black codes allowed plantation workers to coerce black children into unpaid "apprenticeships" without their parents' approval. These practices were outlawed by the Reconstruction legislatures.

The state legislatures also regulated private relations between capital and labor. In some states, merchants paid tenant farmers for the value of their crops only after the merchants had sold the crops and made a profit. State legislatures required up-front payment. Some plantation owners only "paid" ex-slaves in food and tokens for the plantation "shop." Black state legislators passed laws requiring farmers to be paid in cash in order to put an end to this practice.

The Reconstruction state legislatures also contributed to a flourishing of trade unionism (Shofner 1973). The largest of these was the Colored Farmers Alliance, which had 1.25 million members at its peak (Reed 2002:109). The Knights of Labor, the most popular union in the United States, had about sixty thousand black members, making it the first interracial union in US history (Spero and Harris 1959). In some southern states, a majority of trade union members were black. Some of the first strikes in the United States were carried out by black agricultural workers. In 1871, the black community in Perry County, Alabama, organized themselves into the Perry County Labor Union. They collectively threatened to leave the county unless they were given better contacts (Rogers 1970). When faced with intimidation from bosses, Republican state governments sometimes deployed the state militia to support striking black workers.

One of the most radical policy goals of Reconstruction was to redistribute wealth from the slaveholding class to the former slaves. In an age before routinized state cash transfers, the most obvious way to do this was through the redistribution of land.

The first example of land reform came during the Civil War. On his famous "march to the sea" across Georgia, Union general William Sherman found that his army was being followed by thousands of African Americans who had been liberated under the terms of the Emancipation Proclamation. Sherman believed that a clear answer to the growing refugee crisis was to provide land for the ex-slaves to settle. Using forty thousand acres of Confederate land which his army had confiscated, Sherman issued Field Order Number 15, designating forty acres to each black family along the South Carolina and Georgia coasts. The order went down in black lore as "forty acres and a mule."

Once the war was over, Sherman's provisional military order needed sound legal footing. At the federal level, congressman Thaddeus Stevens proposed "to confiscate all the estate of every rebel belligerent whose estate was worth $10,000, or whose land exceeded two hundred acres in quantity." Stevens estimated that this amounted to nearly 400 million acres of land, belonging to about the seventy thousand wealthiest white southerners. "Divide this land into convenient farms. Give, if you please, forty acres to each adult male freedman," Stevens recommended.[13]

Legally speaking, the federal government had already given itself the power to do this in the Confiscation Act of 1862, which authorized "the President of the United States to cause the seizure of all the estate and property" of Confederates. The law clarified, "a person engaged in rebellion, or who has given aid or comfort thereto, the same shall be condemned as enemies' property and become the property of the United States, and may be disposed of as the court shall decree and the proceeds thereof paid into the treasury of the United States." Lincoln had been reluctant to use the law to its fullest extent, although it did form the legal basis of his Emancipation Proclamation, which went into effect five months later. Andrew Johnson's presidency and his blanket pardoning of Confederates rendered the Confiscation Act ineffective, and the ultimate federal effort at land reform was paltry (Bethel 1981).

The failure of land reform for African Americans stands in stark contrast to the scale of capital which the federal government distributed to its white population in the West. Kerri Leigh Merritt (2017: 328) calls the Homestead Act of 1862 "the largest entitlement program in the history of the United States." Over the lifetime of the program, the federal government gave away 246 million acres of public land to 1.6 million white families, who paid little more than a filing fee. By 2000, 46 million people – one in four Americans – were descendants of beneficiaries of the Act.

In contrast, only four thousand black families benefited from the Southern Homestead Act of 1866, which was repealed in 1876 (Oubre 1978). The Act had been intended "to break up Southern aristocracy, prevent speculation, and provide land for Negroes" (Rogers 1970: 7). Yet the flaws in the legislation meant that the vast majority of African Americans entered the twentieth century with no wealth at all. Karlyn Forner (2017) estimates that in Dallas County, Alabama, at the start of the twentieth century, 94 percent of African Americans had no property, forcing them into precarious lives as tenant farmers beholden to white landowners. The failure to make African Americans into landowners, which would have given them crucial and inheritable access to capital and wealth, had severe consequences for material racial inequality and goes some way to explaining the enduring black–white wealth gap. The median white family today is twelve times wealthier than the median black family.

With this failure at the federal level, the majority black state legislature of South Carolina tried its own version of land reform (Bleser 1969). The South Carolina Land Commission, created in 1869, had limited success, but it did provide land to about two thousand black families (perhaps ten thousand people). Ultimately, this project was short-lived and plagued by administrative problems. Nonetheless, the South Carolina land reform project was a demonstration of the creativity and boldness of black state legislators who saw their freedom not just as a matter of legal equality, but also entailing equality in education, labor, and, ultimately – but never completely – capital (land).

Conclusion

The week before Abraham Lincoln died, Richmond, the capital of the Confederacy, was captured by Union troops. One of the companies that took the city was the Massachusetts Fifth Cavalry Regiment, an all-black unit led by the great-grandson of John Adams and grandson of John Quincy Adams, the only two of America's first twelve presidents never to have owned slaves. Rather than let the Union take the city intact, the white residents of Richmond burned it to the ground. According to local legend, slaves assumed the apocalypse was underway as their city burned.

A day after hearing news of Richmond's fall, Lincoln went directly to the city. His journey up the James River was partly thwarted. Dead horses and debris made the journey so treacherous that the president's gunboat was abandoned for a simple row boat. On his arrival in the decimated city, Lincoln was met by the city's black population, who kneeled before him. They called him "Father Abraham." Lincoln balked and told the black Virginians only to kneel before God. Lincoln made his way to the vacated Confederate president's mansion. Upon entering Jefferson Davis's study, Lincoln sat in Davis's chair and asked for a glass of water.

The following week, Lincoln made his famous speech endorsing black voting rights. Four days later, he was dead. In hindsight, Lincoln's death may have done far more for the cause of black suffrage than Lincoln in life may have been prepared to do. Without the conciliatory Lincoln leading the party, Reconstruction was led by his party's radical faction in Congress. They asserted the equal right of all black men to vote, dispatching Lincoln's military and education requirements.

In sum, the core of Reconstruction was a set of statutes and constitutional amendments that provided for the democratization of the United States. Initially, these laws were realized at the national level by Congress alone, but after the 1868 presidential election, they enjoyed support from the Republican administration of Ulysses Grant. Reconstruction laws had brief support from the Supreme Court, but what made these legal reforms meaningful was the willingness of the federal government to use its full coercive power – even the military – to guarantee the citizenship rights of African Americans (Hyman 1997).

The effective coercive muscle flexed by the Military Reconstruction Acts of 1867, the Enforcement Act of 1870, and the Ku Klux Klan Acts of 1871 demonstrated that suppressing racial violence was always a question of political will, not government capacity. When the federal government committed itself to preserving peace and stamping out racist violence, it was broadly able to do so. Some commentators have suggested that, until the late twentieth century, the federal government was "too weak" to provide physical protection to African Americans (Marx 1998). The experience of Reconstruction suggests otherwise.

2

The Fall of the First Reconstruction

The slave went free; stood a brief moment in the sun; then moved back again toward slavery.

W. E. B. Du Bois, *Black Reconstruction in America*
(1935: 26)

Josiah Walls died in obscurity on May 15, 1905. A farm director at Florida Normal College in Tallahassee, Walls's funeral was attended only by his wife and a couple of close acquaintances. His gravesite is unknown, but it is believed that he was buried in the segregated city cemetery.[1] There was no fanfare, no probate will, no obituary, not even a death certificate.

Walls had brought years of agricultural experience to his work at the all-black college, which was later renamed Florida Agricultural and Mechanical University. He had been born a slave in the Shenandoah Valley of Virginia in 1842 and spent the first two decades of his life in bondage, toiling the land. Later in life, he owned an orange farm, consisting of five hundred acres and employing at least fifty farmhands. Before a bad winter ruined him financially, a local newspaper described Walls as living "in one of the finest houses in the county."[2]

Walls had a record of service to his country. During the Civil War, he was forced to work as a slave for the Confederate Army, hauling equipment and digging trenches. He was captured by Union forces at the Battle of Yorktown in 1862 and liberated (Middleton 2002: 357). With his newfound freedom, Walls joined the Third Infantry Regiment of the US Colored Troops. He served with distinction as a sergeant. It is at this time that he is believed to have learned to read (Foner 1993). At the end of the war, Walls's regiment disbanded in Florida, where he chose to settle. He quickly became involved in local politics and joined the Republican Party, like most African Americans who owed their freedom to the party.

The next decade of Walls's life was defined by a series of successful elections. In January 1868, he was elected as a delegate to the post-Civil War Florida state constitutional convention. He was subsequently elected to the Florida state legislature, where he championed legislation barring discrimination against African Americans in hotels and courts. He was credited with being "a spokesman for his race" (Klingman 1976: 29). Another source described him as a "man of considerable ability and moderate demeanor" (Shofner 1974: 180). The reputation served him well, and he was elected mayor of Gainesville, Florida.

Walls's crowning political achievement was his election to the US House of Representatives in 1870. Only eight years earlier, he had been held in bondage as a piece of property with no more rights than livestock. Now, he belonged to the most exclusive and powerful club in the country. Walls represented Florida in Congress for five years, winning three elections.

As a member of Congress, Walls was a vociferous opponent of states' rights and an advocate for national education funding. In a February 1872 debate, he declared:

We know what the cry about state [*sic*] rights means, and more especially when we hear it for the education of the people. Judging from the past, I must confess that I am

somewhat suspicious of such rights, knowing, as I do, that
the Democratic Party ... have been opposed to the education
of the Negro and poor white children.[3]

Walls argued that education was not only necessary for
economic advancement, but also an essential element of
American citizenship. Education could not simply be a state
right. It was a federal responsibility because "education
constitutes the apprenticeship of those who are afterward
to take a place in the order of our civilized and progressive
nation."[4] Walls's dream of substantial federal funding for
schools was not realized for nearly one hundred years, until
the passage of Lyndon Johnson's Elementary and Secondary
Education Act in 1965.

As a congressman, Walls entertained romantic notions of
the multiracial democracy the United States had become.
His final year in office, 1876, was the centennial of the
Declaration of Independence. As Congress was preparing to
mark the anniversary, Walls argued that $3 million should
be appropriated for celebrations in Philadelphia. He told his
fellow representatives:

> [F]ree citizens of a free land shall assemble in the very cradle
> and the place of birth of all that politically they hold dear,
> and exchange with each other the mutual grasp and the
> meaningful glances of a common citizenship ... All questions
> of difference and all harmful recollections will be blotted out.[5]

Walls's vision of a multiracial festivity contrasted with the
reality of the centennial year. He lost his seat to Democrat Jesse
Finley, a former Confederate brigadier general and virulent
white supremacist. As a result of a grubby compromise in
the disputed 1876 presidential election, white leaders in
Walls's own Republican Party agreed to abandon the cause
of Reconstruction, withdrawing the federal presence from
the South and condemning Walls and millions of African
Americans to nearly a century of racialized violence, disenfranchisement, and second-class citizenship.

When Josiah Walls died in 1905, the former congressman could not even vote. There were no black elected officials left in the country. There were only a couple of African Americans clinging on to federal patronage positions and they, too, would be removed from office after the election of the arch-segregationist Woodrow Wilson in 1912 (King 1995). The year before Walls died, the last black woman to hold public office – Minnie Cox, appointed by Republican President Benjamin Harrison – was hounded out of her position. The Democratic governor of Mississippi, James Vardaman, refused to tolerate "a negro wench" as a federal postmistress (Gatewood 1968: 57).[6] She was subjected to formal Senate investigations and eventually fled for her own safety.

The Reconstruction-era state constitutions, which guaranteed equal rights and universal state education, were torn up. Congress formally abolished 94 percent of the voting statutes passed during Reconstruction (Stephenson 1988: 58). An 1893 US House of Representatives committee report vowed: "Let every trace of the reconstruction measures be wiped from the statute books; let the states of this great Union understand that the elections are in their own hands." The Reconstruction amendments – banning slavery, guaranteeing equal citizenship, barring racial discrimination in voting – remained in the Constitution but only as dead letters, rendered useless by presidents and congresses that refused to enforce them, and a Supreme Court that said they could not.

* * *

The tragic life of Josiah Walls is a window into the wider forces of democratization and de-democratization in nineteenth-century America along racial lines. The unfathomability of a former slave becoming a congressman is matched by the incomprehension of a former congressman dying without the right to vote. Reconstruction was a clear example of democratic expansion. This chapter explains why the United States then underwent a severe episode of democratic reversal. The first section explores the variety of historical arguments proffered to explain Reconstruction's collapse. I ultimately argue that the First Reconstruction was undone by hostile, elite actors enabled by anti-democratic institutions embedded in the US Constitution, which led to extreme state-level violence that went unchallenged politically due to the failure to generate cross-party consensus for civil rights. The next three sections of this chapter unpack each component of my argument.

It is worth noting that I do not date the end of Reconstruction with the 1876 presidential election, as many authors do (Shofner 1974; Foner 1988). The shameful Compromise of 1877, which saw the national Republican Party agree to withdraw federal presence from the South in exchange for electoral college votes, did not put an immediate end to multiracial politics in the region. African American politicians continued to get elected in the South, in diminishing numbers, until the very end of the nineteenth century. Instead, federal departure led to a "war of attrition" for black voting rights in the states (Valelly 2016). It is important not to overlook the black political activists and radical Republicans who struggled for a generation after the national Republican Party effectively closed up shop on civil rights.

The grassroots struggle bore some fruit. In the 1890s, there was a brief resurgence of multiracial politics with pro-civil rights "fusion" tickets of working-class white populists and black Republicans challenging the elite-dominated, white supremacist Democrats. Tremendous violence and state-level corruption snuffed out these activities. Legitimately elected politicians were murdered or driven out of their seats by white supremacists, who then replaced them in what amounted to political coups. Under the guise of states' rights, the federal government sat on its hands as the physical infrastructure of Reconstruction's multiracial democracy – black churches, local Republican Party headquarters, newspaper offices – quite literally burned. By the start of the twentieth century, Reconstruction was finally dead.

For the next half a century, the South existed under one-party rule, not due to broad electoral support but as a consequence of state actions to whittle down the electorate to a manageable size that could be controlled by an elite, racially homogenous minority. Robert Mickey (2015) describes these shrunken electorates as "authoritarian enclaves," and the phenomenon has been noted by comparative political scientists in other federal systems (Behrend and Whitehead 2016). Given the institutional power and advantages that these authoritarian elites held in national American politics, I argue that it is impossible to describe the United States as a whole as resembling anything like a full democracy until black voting rights were restored by the Voting Rights Act of 1965.

Theories Explaining the End of the First Reconstruction

Traditional accounts of the failure of the First Reconstruction pointed their fingers at two culprits. The first consisted of the white Republican members of Congress who were part of their party's radical faction. Out of a combination of reckless, ideological zeal and partisan ambition, the authors of sweeping civil rights legislation from 1865 to 1875 were said to have acted too "hastily," placing institutional change ahead of public opinion (Myrdal 1944). According to this account, ordinary whites were simply not prepared to share power with African Americans. In a country that had hitherto viewed citizenship as having an inherently white character, the failure to build deep public support among whites for black civil rights before legislating such rights doomed the project of Reconstruction from the start (Frymer 2017; Bateman 2018; Immerwahr 2019). A more incremental approach, in line with gradual change in public opinion, would have been more successful (Hackney 1969).

The problem with this account is that it is not obvious that the mass white electorate was inherently hostile to African American incorporation in the public sphere. The brief explosion of multiracial populism in the southern states in the 1890s suggests an alternative path. One of the perennial mistakes made by liberals is to worry about the "tyranny of the majority," but elite minorities are more likely than mass electorates to pose greater dangers to democracy (Bermeo 2003). The regimes of white supremacist racial segregation, known as Jim Crow, were predicated on the shrinking of the eligible electorate – not only African Americans but also poor whites. For example, only 8 percent of Virginian adults on average voted in statewide elections in the 1920s–40s in a state that was 75 percent white (Sabato 1978: 110).

The second strand of scholarship blamed African Americans themselves. These accounts argued that the black population was simply unprepared to go from the legal status of property, to full citizens, to voters, to elected officials – all within half a decade. The school of thought, associated with the historian William Dunning, argued that Reconstruction failed due to black "misrule." African Americans got drunk off the spoils of war, credulously fell prey to the poor guidance of white radicals, and led their states to fiscal and economic ruin (Dunning 1907; Fleming 1919; Coulter 1947).

Even northern politicians and academics indulged in this slander. Charles Frances Adams, a descendent of the two Presidents Adams, described black officeholding in 1908 as "worse than a crime" and lamented "the promiscuous conferring of the ballot" to African Americans.[7] Hilary Herbert (1901) wrote in the *Annals of the American Academy of Political and Social Science*: "The granting of universal suffrage to the Negro was the mistake of the nineteenth century. I say that believing myself to be a friend to the Negro." President William Taft, a supposed racial moderate and leader of the party of Lincoln, argued: "There is no constitutional right in anyone to hold office. A one-legged man would hardly be suited for a mail carrier and, although, we deplore his misfortune, nevertheless, we would not seek to neutralize it by giving him a place that he could not fill."[8] Taft sacked Dr. William Crum, the black customs inspector in Charleston, purely because he was black.[9] "This is first-rate," Taft's Republican predecessor Theodore Roosevelt cheered, when he heard that Crum had gone without a fuss.[10] These sentiments were promoted widely in popular culture. Charles Bower's 1929 best-seller *The Tragic Era*, Thomas Dixon's 1905 play *The Clansman*, and D. W. Griffith's landmark 1915 film *The Birth of a Nation* all portrayed black officeholders as corrupt and flamboyant, brought down by their own excesses.

This explanation entails a breathtaking absolution of white officials from the sustained campaigns of violence and unremitting political opposition that were directed toward African Americans. It further relies on blatantly racist tropes about black incompetence, which black elected officials continue to face today. These accounts were subjected to staunch criticism by the black social scientist W. E. B. Du Bois in his 1935 masterpiece *Black Reconstruction in America*. Du Bois sarcastically summarized the historiography: "All Negroes were ignorant; all Negroes were lazy and extravagant; Negroes were responsible for bad government during Reconstruction" (1935: 711–12). Ignored and derided by contemporaries for unfair reasons such as limited archival research – impossible for a black man during segregation – Du Bois's counternarrative has been taken up by more recent historians and stands tall in comparison to the now much-repudiated other histories of Reconstruction published in the first half of the twentieth century.

Some historians have looked to economic factors to explain Reconstruction's demise (Richardson 2001). As was discussed in the previous chapter, the failure to redistribute wealth was a major unfulfilled promise of Reconstruction. The massive transfer of public land and, therefore, wealth to white families in the western United States during the nineteenth century was not matched for black families, with enduring and compounding consequences for material racial inequality. Nonetheless, the failure of wealth redistribution is not sufficient to explain Reconstruction's failure. It was a policy consequence of the weak durability of Reconstruction, not a cause of the weakness itself.

Other commentators argue that Reconstruction failed due to the weak capacity of the central state in nineteenth-century America. Paul Frymer (1999: 86), for example, writes that "the federal government lacked the capacity to deal with such an enormous undertaking." The position of uniform state weakness, however, is hard to maintain when one considers the multiple instances of undeniable state strength in the nineteenth-century United States, as Kimberley Johnson (2016) has pointed out. Among these, we can include Native American "removal" and tribal administration (Rockwell 2010), slavery's enforcement and anti-refugee policies (Lubet 2010), colonial administration (Immerwahr 2019), and national regulations of religious practices (Gordon 2002; Novkov 2014). Theda Skocpol and Kenneth Finegold (Skocpol and Finegold 1982: 271) were right to see "islands of state strength" throughout American history. This has been particularly true in regard to policing race relations. When the central US state has sought to impose its will domestically, more often than not, it has been able to do so.

Instead, this chapter makes an institutionalist argument about democratic backsliding in the United States. Plagued by a constitution that contains numerous undemocratic elements, the United States is susceptible to democratic reversal by agents willing to exploit these institutions on behalf of privileged minorities. The Supreme Court, the electoral college, and federalism provided white racists with structural advantages that enabled them to roll back democratic reforms legislated by Congress. These anti-democratic actors were enabled by a failure of political will to resist them. Racially polarized partisanship meant that it was to the clear political advantage of one party (the Democrats) to undermine the black franchise, whereas the efforts by the party overwhelmingly supported by blacks (the Republicans) to expand and protect black suffrage were treated with immense suspicion by whites. Ultimately, the risk of white voters defecting from the Republican coalition to the Democrats was enough to constrain national Republican politicians from making little more than piecemeal and symbolic gestures to their black electorate.

Judicial Deconstruction

The collapse of Reconstruction was not due to federal passivity. Reconstruction was actively deconstructed. No institution was more nefarious and destructive than the US Supreme Court. For most of US history, the Supreme Court has sided with privileged minorities while excluding the poor and racial minorities from political power. With few exceptions, the court has actively thwarted and rolled back democratic progress. Baby boomer liberals who have dominated US legal academia in recent years are overly influenced by the exceptional example of the Warren Court (1953–69), which operated as a democratizing force.[11] This outlier has led many, mistakenly, to see the Supreme Court as the key democratic, rights-preserving institution in the federal government.

Yet, in the same century as the Warren Court, the Supreme Court crippled efforts to give economic power to the working class (*Lochner v. New York*, 1905), blocked the federal government from regulating industry (*US v. E. C. Knight Co*, 1895), ruled redistributive taxation unconstitutional (*Pollock v. Farmers' Loan and Trust Co.*, 1895),[12] and attempted to strangle the nascent Roosevelt welfare state in its crib (*Schechter Poultry Corporation v. US*, 1935). Had Franklin Roosevelt not threatened to use his huge democratic majorities (small-d and large-D) to strip the court of its power, there may have been no durable New Deal welfare state. More recently, the Supreme Court has shown itself to be an unapologetic ally of moneyed minorities (*Citizens United v. FEC*, 2010), further impairing Congress's attempts to protect the key democratic principle of equal influence in American elections and governance.

Before the Civil War, the Supreme Court regularly supported the elite, minority slaveholding interest against states, which tried to protect black civil rights (Crowe 2010). The court forced abolitionist state officials to execute pro-slavery federal laws; in some cases, state laws designed to protect African Americans were invalidated. In *Prigg v. Pennsylvania* (1842), the court invalidated Pennsylvania statutes designed to protect runaway slaves, forcing the abolitionist and traditionally Quaker state to turn over escaped slaves to federal authorities. In *Ableman v. Booth* (1859), the court sided with the national government against the state of Wisconsin, which tried to provide legal protection to abolitionists who sheltered ex-slaves. These cases complicate the usual narrative that Reconstruction failed because the Supreme Court was inherently oriented toward states' rights. When states were agents of abolitionism, the Supreme Court sided with a strong central government to enforce a nationwide anti-fugitive slave regime.

The Supreme Court's interventions meant that no black person was truly "free" in the pre-Civil War United States. In *Dred Scott v. Sandford* (1857), the court even argued that it was a legal impossibility for any black person to be a US citizen. Pointing out that the country was founded to protect white interests, Chief Justice Roger Taney wrote,

> [I]n the eyes and thoughts of the men who framed the Declaration of Independence and established the State Constitutions and Governments[, t]hey show that a perpetual and impassable barrier was intended to be erected between the white race and the one which they had reduced to slavery ... no distinction in this respect was made between the free negro or mulatto and the slave.

The First Reconstruction was no exception to the Supreme Court's long, malevolent history as an institution sheltering racist, anti-democratic actors. When people begin to learn about Reconstruction, they are sometimes surprised to discover that Congress first guaranteed black voting rights in 1866 and abolished segregation on public transport and in accommodations in 1875. People are familiar with the equivalent legislation of 1964 and 1965, presuming them to be the first of their kind. The reason that these earlier civil rights laws did not survive into the twentieth century was due to sustained attacks from the Supreme Court, which eventually ruled them unconstitutional.

The failure to disable the Supreme Court's powerful position within the US Constitution was a key mistake of the radical Republicans. It left their democratization project extremely vulnerable to attack and reversal. Their error may have been due to a false sense of security. Perhaps not coincidentally, when the pro-civil rights reformers were at their greatest strength in Congress, the court appeared supportive of Reconstruction (*White v. Texas* 1869).[13] Radicals miscalculated that once their influence in Congress waned, the Supreme Court would remain supportive of the civil rights agenda.

One of the strongest supporters of the Reconstruction amendments was the Lincoln-appointed Chief Justice Salmon Chase (White 1993). In the circuit court case *In re Turner* (1867), Chase overturned the *Dred Scott* decision, stating: "Colored persons equally with white persons are citizens of the United States." Chase's ruling came a year before the Fourteenth Amendment, showing that he believed that the Civil War and the liberation of slaves had fundamentally readjusted the meaning of American citizenship. His jurisprudence did not endure: he suffered a stroke in 1870, which restricted his participation on the court, and he died three years later. After Chase's stroke, the Supreme Court pursued a relentless path of deconstructing Reconstruction (see Table 2.1). The Supreme Court minimized the Union victory, contorted the meaning of the Reconstruction amendments until they were effectively immobilized, and struck down some of the most important civil rights legislation in US history.

Chase died three weeks after dissenting in the first major judicial attack against the democratic legal infrastructure of Reconstruction: the *Slaughterhouse Cases* of 1873. The facts of the cases had nothing to do with black civil rights, but the

Table 2.1: Judicial deconstruction

Case	Year	Majority	President	Content
Slaughterhouse Cases	1873	5–4	Ulysses Grant (R)	The Fourteenth Amendment does not limit states from depriving citizens of their civil rights
US v. Cruikshank	1876	5–4	Ulysses Grant (R)	The Fourteenth Amendment does not give Congress the power to outlaw private acts of racial discrimination
US v. Reese	1876	7–2	Ulysses Grant (R)	The Fifteenth Amendment does not provide a positive right to vote
Civil Rights Cases	1883	8–1	Chester Arthur (R)	The Civil Rights Act of 1875 is unconstitutional; Congress cannot stop businesses from discriminating against customers based on race
Plessy v. Ferguson	1896	7–1	Grover Cleveland (D)	"Separate but equal" (racial segregation) is constitutional
Williams v. Mississippi	1898	9–0	William McKinley (R)	Devices such as the poll tax, literacy test, and grandfather clause are constitutional, even if in practice they are discriminatory
Giles v. Teasley	1904	6–3	Theodore Roosevelt (R)	The court cannot compel a state to enforce the Fifteenth Amendment
Berea College v. Kentucky	1908	7–2	William Taft (R)	States can force private institutions to implement racial segregation against their will

court's decision had profound – and lethal – implications for African Americans. A group of butchers sued the state of Louisiana for requiring them to work in municipally owned abattoirs for the sake of public health. New Orleans butchers argued that the closure of private abattoirs was a violation of "the privileges or immunities of citizens of the United States," which the Fourteenth Amendment protected.[14]

On Easter Monday 1873, in the Old Senate Chamber of the US Capitol, Justice Samuel Miller read out the 5–4 majority opinion that he had authored. He argued that the butchers had no grounds in their case against the state of Louisiana because the Fourteenth Amendment only protected a very limited number of federal rights. These were the sort of rights that pertained specifically to citizens' relationship to the government in Washington – the right to petition a federal official for redress of grievance, the right "to the sub-treasuries, land offices, and courts of justice," and "the right to use the navigable waters of the United States." Other rights, including the butchers' right to operate a private abattoir, "must rest for their security and protection where they have heretofore rested" – the states.

Citing pre-Civil War jurisprudence, Miller explained that "the entire domain of civil rights heretofore belong[ed] exclusively to the States." It was true that in 1833 the Supreme Court had ruled in *Barron v. Baltimore* that states were allowed to deprive citizens of the kinds of rights found in the Bill of Rights of the US Constitution. For example, the First Amendment reads: "Congress shall make no law respecting an establishment of religion, or prohibiting the free exercise thereof; or abridging the freedom of speech, or of the press; or the right of the people peaceably to assemble, and to petition the government for a redress of grievances." According to the principle of "dual federalism" established in *Barron*, these rights still could be deprived legitimately by state governments. Congress could not prohibit freedom of speech or press, but a state legislature could. In 1830, the state of North Carolina passed a statute that criminalized public dissent of slavery. The state also made it illegal to publish any writings that encouraged "free negroes to be dissatisfied with their social condition." Those found in violation of the law were subject to public whipping, being put in the pillory, or a year in prison. Repeat offenders could be put to death. In 1860, the state legislature revised the law and authorized execution for first offenders.

In his opinion in the *Slaughterhouse Cases*, Miller dishonestly claimed that the Fourteenth Amendment had "not radically changed the whole theory of the relations of the State and Federal governments to each other ... We are convinced that no such results were intended by the Congress which proposed these amendments." This was a shockingly dishonest interpretation of the Fourteenth Amendment, which had been written by the radical Republicans with the clear intention of nationalizing, standardizing, and centralizing citizenship rights to protect African Americans. As a Fifth Circuit judge had recognized two years earlier in the case *US v. Hall*, "by the original constitution, citizenship in the United States was a consequence of citizenship in a state. By this clause [the Fourteenth Amendment], this order of things is reversed."

While Miller ostensibly ruled against the white Louisiana butchers, who were represented by the former Confederate Secretary of War, the impact of his opinion was a firm victory for the wider forces of white supremacy. The Supreme Court had effectively declared that most civil rights were matters purely for state regulation; the federal government could not protect them. The court's ruling in the *Slaughterhouse Cases* resurrected the fiction of dual citizenship, as if the Civil War and Reconstruction amendments had never happened.

On the very same day that Miller delivered this legal blow to black civil rights, well over a hundred black political activists in Grant Parish, Louisiana – about 220 miles north of New Orleans – lay dead or maimed. In the 1872 elections, African Americans in Grant Parish, who formed a bare majority, succeeded in electing Republicans to the parish roles of judge and sheriff.[15] Local white Democrats disputed the results, but they were confirmed as legitimate by the governor. In late March 1873, the new Republican officials took their public oaths in the courthouse of the county seat, Colfax. In many parts of the South, the federal army would have been deployed to protect these officials, but due to Colfax's remoteness, federal troops were unavailable. Instead, the local sheriff and judge were protected by a band of black militiamen who dug trenches around the courthouse and kept constant guard to protect, both symbolically and physically, the election results. At noon on Easter Sunday, the losing white Democrats decided to seize control of the courthouse.

Bill Cruikshank, one of the leaders, ordered his former slave Pinckney Chambers to approach the courthouse with a lit ball of cloth and set the building on fire. If Chambers didn't obey, he would be shot. Chambers miserably approached the courthouse and set it alight. Upon his return, Cruikshank told Chambers, "You're a good old nigger" and promised him safe return home. "If you're good, he'll keep you as a pet," one of the white terrorists chimed (Lane 2008: 101). Recognizing that resistance would be futile, the freedmen surrendered, complying with orders to leave their guns in the burning courthouse. They exited, waving handkerchiefs in the air as tokens of surrender. As they walked outside, they were gunned down by the white Democrats. Survivors were captured as prisoners and taken onto the banks of the Red River, where they were shot. The river earned its name that Easter day as bodies were ignominiously thrown into it. Estimates of how many black Republicans were killed vary, ranging from sixty to eighty.[16]

The newly installed white Democratic lawmakers had no interest in prosecuting the murderers for their crime. Indeed, the lawmakers themselves had been participants. The federal government stepped in, using the Enforcement Act of 1870 and Fourteenth Amendment as their legal basis. The Enforcement Act empowered US attorneys to prosecute common law crimes (such as murder) if they were part of an anti-civil rights conspiracy. In order to convict the ringleaders of the Colfax Massacre, the federal government needed to establish that the civil rights of the murdered and maimed black activists were being violated. Given the circumstances, this should have been a straightforward task. The US attorney identified thirty civil rights violations in the case, which became *US v. Cruikshank*.

In oral argument before the Supreme Court, the black citizens of Colfax were represented by President Grant's attorney general George Williams. Williams pointed out the Supreme Court's historic hypocrisy in siding with states' rights in matters of white supremacy but obviating them when they tended toward black equality. The attorney general told the justices:

> [T]he original constitution recognized the right of the slave-holder to property in his slaves and the Supreme Court decided that Congress had the right to pass a law to protect him in those rights. If the time ever comes when as liberal a construction shall be given to laws designed to protect human freedom as has always been given to laws designed to protect human slavery, then the doctrine of the government in this case would be admitted.

Williams argued that the Reconstruction amendments had done exactly that. He concluded his plea to the justices: "I look forward to the day when we can consider ourselves not a nation of inharmonious and warring sovereigns, but a Union whose broad shield shall protect – in all and every right of a freeman and a citizen – her people from one end to the other."

The court's opinion in *US v. Cruikshank*, written by Chief Justice Morrison Waite, was nearly five thousand words long. Astonishingly, not once did it mention that dozens of African Americans had been slaughtered at the Colfax courthouse on Easter Sunday 1873. Waite declared that the Fourteenth Amendment "adds nothing to the rights of citizen as against another ... The duty of protecting all its citizens in the enjoyment of an equality of rights was originally assumed by the States, and it still remains there." He delivered the fatal blow: "[S]overeignty, for the protection of the rights of life and personal liberty within the respective States, rests alone with the States." The Enforcement Act of 1870 was rendered effectively inoperable. The federal government could not intervene to protect African Americans being shot and killed by white assailants for their race and political beliefs.

After depleting the Fourteenth Amendment of meaningful value, the Supreme Court turned its attention to congressional civil rights statutes. In its line of sight was the federal ban on segregation. In the 1874 midterm elections, the Republicans were decisively routed by the Democrats. They lost 93 out of 293 seats in the House of Representatives. It was the Republicans' worst defeat in American history. In the Senate, the Democrats gained nine additional states. Seeing the writing on the wall for Reconstruction, in the lame-duck session, the Republicans passed one final piece of civil rights legislation. The Civil Rights Act of 1875 was signed into law by Ulysses Grant three days before the expiration of the 44th Congress. The legislation outlawed segregation in public spaces. Specifically, it stated:

> [A]ll persons within the jurisdiction of the United States shall be entitled to the full and equal enjoyment of the accommodations, advantages, facilities, and privileges of inns, public conveyances on land or water, theaters, and other places of public amusement ... applicable alike to citizens of every race and color, regardless of any previous condition of servitude.

Over the next few years, multiple African Americans sued businesses that fell afoul of this law. These cases made their way through the federal court system and arrived at the docket of the Supreme Court in the early 1880s. Two cases involved black patrons being denied a hotel room; two involved theaters; one involved public transport. They included northern states as well as southern states. One plaintiff had been denied a seat in Maguire's Theatre in San Francisco; another had been denied a ticket in the Grand

Opera House in New York. One of the plaintiffs was a black woman who had been denied entry to a women's railway carriage.

The justices decided to issue one ruling applying to all of these cases, known collectively as the *Civil Rights Cases*, in 1883. Justice Joseph Bradley, who wrote the opinion of the court, was a longstanding opponent of the Civil Rights Act of 1875. After its passage, he had sputtered:

> To deprive white people of the right of choosing their own company would be to introduce another kind of slavery ... It can never be endured that the white shall be compelled to lodge and eat and sit with the Negro ... The antipathy of race cannot be crushed and annihilated by legal enactment. (Cushman 2013: 182)

In his decision in the *Civil Rights Cases*, Bradley finally was able to reverse this legal enactment. The court struck down the Civil Rights Act of 1875 as unconstitutional. The Reconstruction amendments, the court reasoned, had not made racial prejudice illegal. If a business owner wished to refuse service to an African American or force a black person to sit in a separate space, it was not within the power of the federal government to do anything about it. This was a devastating decision. It destroyed what turned out to be the last civil rights law passed by Congress until the 1950s.

The final judicial nail in the coffin of Reconstruction was the Supreme Court's ruling in *Plessy v. Ferguson* (1896). Because the Supreme Court enjoys constitutional supremacy in the US system, it can act as a nationalizing agent more easily than any other institution. In some instances, the Supreme Court has nationalized rights: for example, abortion (*Roe v. Wade*, 1973) and same-sex marriage (*Obergfell v. Hodges*, 2015). But, the court can also use its sweeping authority to authorize discrimination across the United States. In *Plessy v. Ferguson*, the court embraced the constitutionality of *de jure* racial discrimination. Separate facilities, the court disastrously argued, were not in violation of the Fourteenth Amendment's equal protection requirements because "separate" implied only difference, not inequality.

The system of "checks and balances" in the United States made it easier for hostile actors to evade responsibility for acts of de-democratization. The Supreme Court has long engaged in a strategy of shifting responsibility to other institutions. One appalling example at the end of the First Reconstruction was the case *Giles v. Teasley* in 1904. Justice Oliver Wendell Holmes recognized that the new white supremacist constitution of Alabama was a flagrant violation of the Reconstruction amendments, but he claimed that overturning those provisions was not the responsibility of the court. Holmes stated bluntly: "We are dealing with a new and extraordinary situation ... [in which] the whole registration scheme of the Alabama constitution is a fraud upon the Constitution of the United States," but he claimed that a Supreme Court decision could not overturn this flagrantly unconstitutional document because it was a non-justiciable, political matter. Holmes lamented that "the great mass of the white population intends to keep the blacks from voting ... a name on a piece of paper [i.e., a Supreme Court decision] will not defeat them. Unless we are prepared to supervise the voting in that state by officers of the court," then there was no point striking down the racist state constitution.

Holmes explained that redress for the violation of civil rights did not lie with the Supreme Court but with Congress and the president. He stated: "[R]elief from a great political wrong, if done, as alleged, by the people of a state and the state itself, must be given by them or by the legislative and political department of the government of the United States." Holmes knew full well that neither the president nor Congress would act, leaving African Americans disenfranchised by the state's white supremacist post-Reconstruction constitution until Congress finally intervened with the Voting Rights Act sixty years later.

Violence in the States

In the comparative political science literature, when democracies fall, violent, anti-democratic insurgencies are often to blame. The nineteenth-century United States was characterized by multiple violent insurrections designed to topple legitimately elected local and state governments and to crush political opposition through intimidation and force. As Reconstruction failed, top-level institutions continued to function "as normal." Presidential elections continued to happen on time. The stars and stripes were not replaced with the stars and bars. For many Americans, there was little discernible change.

However, quietly (to whites, in any case) democracy in the United States was being dismantled. Multiple US states fell to anti-democratic coups. Public officials who did not subscribe to the new regime of white supremacy were murdered, removed from office, or made into political refugees. Voters were terrorized and blocked from voting or standing for office. The physical infrastructure of the multiracial democratic sphere – black churches, schools, and printing presses – were burnt to the ground. Rightfully elected public officials were blocked from taking office. Anywhere else in the world, these acts would be viewed as hallmarks of a violent overthrow of democracy, and we should apply the same standard to the United States.

The strategy of violence to undermine Reconstruction operated at multiple levels. First, there were the high-profile assassinations. The biggest of these prizes was, of course, President Abraham Lincoln. But, many other elected officials were murdered by political opponents. The period saw the first assassination of a sitting congressman: the pro-civil rights James Hinds was shot dead in the street by the secretary of his county Democratic Party. One of the key architects of Georgia's Reconstruction constitution was murdered in his bedroom by the Ku Klux Klan (Daniell 1975).

While records are patchy, among African American elected officials during Reconstruction, at least twelve state legislators, eight state constitutional convention delegates, and one state party chair were assassinated (Foner 1993). The Ku Klux Klan and other white supremacist groups effectively operated as paramilitaries of the Democratic Party. Democratic activists and Klan members were often indistinguishable in some parts of the South. As Keeanga-Yamahtta Taylor (2008) writes: "When they [Democrats] could not win the vote, they simply shot and killed Black officials and replaced them with white men."

The assassinations were designed to intimidate officeholders and deter others from standing for election. The credible threats of murder and maiming by white Democrats forced Republican politicians to resign and flee their states, moving to the North as political refugees. At least three Republican governors were disposed of in this way. After the Ku Klux Klan garroted to death a Republican state senator in the Caswell County Courthouse, William Holden, the governor of North Carolina, deployed the state militia to restore order and ensure the security of the local African American population. In response, Holden was impeached by the Democratic state legislature – the first removal of a governor by impeachment in US history – and was forced to flee North Carolina for his own life (Kousser 1984). In a similar set of circumstances, Adelbert Ames, the Republican governor of Mississippi, resigned under threat of violence in 1876 and fled to Minnesota. The Democratic state legislature first impeached Ames's black lieutenant governor to ensure that Ames was not replaced by an African American (Anderson 1981).

The violence also had a policy impact. Whites who were sympathetic to black political inclusion began to withdraw their support out of fear of deathly repercussions. This was shamefully exhibited in the Georgia state legislature, when some white Republicans joined with Democrats to vote to expel all thirty-three African American members of the legislature. Around this time, the Republican governor of Georgia, Rufus Bollock, was pressured by the Ku Klux Klan to resign. He fled to the North, fearing for his life. White

Republicans became increasingly hesitant to support black civil rights out of fear of violent political retribution.

This elite-level violence only hinted at the extreme violence targeted toward ordinary party activists, especially black Republicans. Almost as soon as the Civil War was over, whites engaged in mass killings of African Americans. The Freedmen's Bureau in 1866 estimated that in the one year it took before establishing itself in Texas, one thousand blacks had been murdered in retaliatory violence by whites. In July 1866, thirty-eight black political activists were gunned down by local white police in New Orleans (Hogue 2006). In reaction to the presence of black federal soldiers in Memphis in 1866, a white riot erupted: the mob murdered forty-six black residents, raped five black women, and burned all twelve of Memphis's black schools, four black churches, and ninety-one homes. The head of the Secret Service Hiram Whitley estimated that "23,000 persons, black and white, were scourged or murdered by the Ku Klux Klan within 10 years following the close of the rebellion."[17]

Violence was most manifest around elections, under-scoring the political (and fundamentally anti-democratic) dimension of these actions. In the 1869 municipal elections in Mobile, Alabama, white Democrats wheeled out a piece of field artillery and trained it on a large crowd of African Americans who were queuing to cast their votes. The *Alabama State Journal* outrageously described the crowd as "timid," because "hundreds left the place as fast as possible."[18] In the 1874 elections in the same city, white horsemen rode through the streets shooting black men who were on their way to the polls.[19] Across the South, party activists' bodies could be found drowned in rivers or hanging from trees. Because voting was not secret (and would not be in some southern states until the 1950s), any person who dared to vote Republican could easily be singled out. In one Louisiana parish, in the face of threats from white Democrats, (only) one individual cast his vote for Republican candidate Ulysses Grant. He was murdered that night (Christensen 2012).

White terrorist violence was not limited to election day. Any expression of black power was met with violent resistance. This became much worse when the federal government withdrew its presence from the South, leaving African Americans to the mercy of white mob justice. More than two thousand black men were lynched after the federal government departed the South in 1876 (Kato 2015). Between 1885 and 1907, there were more lynchings than legal executions in the United States (Whitfield 1988: 101).

In 1887, black sugarcane workers in Thibodaux, Louisiana, went on strike. The laborers were paid in "tokens" that could only be redeemed in the plantation shop owned by their employer. The farmers were members of the racially mixed Knights of Labor, the biggest union in American history. One in five American workers were members of the Knights at the time, double the proportion of Americans today who are a member of all unions put together. Cognizant of the farmers' collective potential, the plantation owners sought to suppress the strike as robustly as possible. They hired white strike-breakers to attack the black sharecroppers; about fifty were murdered as a result. One plantation owner mused: "I think this will settle the question of who is to rule – the nigger or the white man – for the next fifty years" (DeSantis 2016). It was sufficient to kill off most attempts to unionize black sharecroppers until the Second Reconstruction, with the exception of the Communist-led unions in the 1910s–30s, whose efforts were similarly met with murderous response (see Gilmore 2008).[20]

The Supreme Court was partner to these dreadful acts of anti-democratic violence. Two years after the Civil Rights Act of 1866 became law, a former slave family in Kentucky was assaulted in a nighttime attack by two white Democratic activists. John Blyew and George Kennard had just come from a Democratic Party meeting, convinced that there "would soon be another war about the niggers." They entered the black family's cabin and hacked to death Sallie Foster, her husband Jack, and her 97-year-old, blind mother Lucy Armstrong. Even though Blyew and Kennard had sliced off his hands, Jack Foster tried to drag himself to help before dying in a pool of blood at the door. The Fosters' 16-year-old son Richard crawled in agonizing pain for ninety minutes to alert a neighbor. He died of his horrific injuries two days later, but not before giving a formal witness statement. Blyew and Kennard also attacked the Fosters' 6-year-old daughter, swinging an axe across her head and disfiguring her for life. Only 8-year-old Laura Foster survived without physical harm.

The case was heard in a federal court. Kentucky state law did not allow blacks to testify against whites, and the lower-tier federal court accepted that the Fosters were "denied the right to testify" against Blyew and Kennard "solely on account of race and color." Based on the testimony of the late Richard Foster and his elder surviving sister, Blyew and Kennard were convicted each to "hang ... by the neck until he is dead." This was an extremely significant ruling. Before the Civil Rights Act of 1866, it was unheard of for white men to be sentenced to death for killing black people.

The defendants appealed the verdict, and the case was sent to the Supreme Court. The defendants' attorney Jeremiah Black compared his clients to the apostle Paul who was taken to trial by "a set of pagan scallawags and carpetbag Jews." In an utterly astonishing move, the Supreme Court reversed the convictions. The court interpreted the Civil Rights Act to apply federal jurisdiction only in cases where an African American was a plaintiff or defendant. Since neither party in the case (i.e., the state of Kentucky or Blyew and Kennard) was black, the court decided there was no question of discrimination and, therefore, no reason for the trial to be held in a federal court. The court acknowledged that the victims of the murder were all black, but, since they were dead, their race was "beyond" the court's consideration.

The case returned to Kentucky to be heard in the state court. The initial trial resulted in a hung jury. By the time a conviction was decided, John Blyew had mysteriously escaped. Neither man was sentenced to death. In the 1890s, the governor of Kentucky pardoned both of them, Blyew having served no time in prison at all. They both survived into the twentieth century, with George Kennard living until a ripe old age before passing away in 1923.

Racially Polarized Partisanship

Although the Supreme Court, the electoral college, and federalism enabled hostile minorities to attack civil rights, the damage done by these anti-democratic institutions could have been minimized. There are sufficient democratic features in the US Constitution to enable elected actors with a strong political will to prevail, but the undertaking is enormous. The Reconstruction Congress and the Grant administration, working together, demonstrated this powerfully. Equally, they showed the inherent instability of a political response without sufficient structural reform. In this case, political will was not maintained in part because civil rights became a highly partisan issue.

The First Reconstruction had lopsided political backing, which rendered it extremely vulnerable. Race and people's attitudes on race were strongly connected to party support. In the South, where this phenomenon was most pronounced, nearly all African Americans voted Republican, while a large majority of whites voted Democratic. Every effort to protect black voting rights was viewed with partisan suspicion. Gideon Welles, a Republican who became a skeptic of Reconstruction, wrote: "It is evident that intense partisanship instead of philanthropy is the root of the movement" (quoted in Woodward 1957: 235).

The intense partisan loyalty of African Americans to the Republican Party was ultimately dangerous for Reconstruction because Democrats saw little reason to make appeals to African American voters. Their emotional attachment to the party of Lincoln was unshakable. Ex-slave and abolitionist Frederick Douglass captured this perspective when he wrote in 1883: "For the life of me I cannot see how any honest colored man who has brains enough to put two ideas together can allow himself under the notion of independence to give aid and comfort to the Democratic party."[21]

Wanting to see how deep these loyalties went, in 2014 I interviewed 94-year-old Republican Edward Brooke, who was born and raised in segregated Washington, DC, and who had been the first black US senator since the First Reconstruction. The Republican Party by that time had moved away from Brooke's own liberal social and pro-civil rights policy positions (Johnson 2018). I asked him why he did not leave the party. He protested that he could not do so because it was the party that had given his ex-slave grandfather – whom Brooke remembered – freedom.[22] This is not to say that a man of Brooke's intellect was a Republican simply because his grandfather was. Joshua Farrington is right to say that commentators should avoid reducing post-Reconstruction black Republicans to "elderly partisans clutching to hallowed memories of Abraham Lincoln" (2016: 3). Nonetheless, Brooke's emotional attachment to the Republican Party as the "party of emancipation" was real and still evident 150 years after abolition. It puts in context the intensity of the tribal loyalty that many ex-slaves felt to the Republicans in the nineteenth century, which no policy offer from the Democrats could easily dislodge.

Congressman George White was the last African American remaining in Congress when he strode to the lectern of the House of Representatives in January 1901. Already a lame duck, White had chosen not to contest the 1900 elections out of a sense of futility and fear of further violence. His final speech in Congress is one of the most important and powerful ever delivered in that legislature. White decried the horrific conditions which African Americans had endured in the years after slavery: "[L]ynching, burning at the stake, with the humiliation of Jim Crow laws, the disfranchisement of our male citizens, slander and degradation of our women, with the factories closed against us." White chastised the white representatives for mocking the poor social condition of the country's black population: "After enforced debauchery with many kindred horrors incident to slavery, it comes with ill grace from the perpetrators of these deeds to hold up the shortcomings of some of our race to ridicule and scorn." White, then, concluded on a note of defiance, which continues to resonate today:

> Mr. Chairman, before concluding my remarks I want to submit a brief recipe for the solution of the so-called "American Negro problem." He asks no special favors, but simply demands that he be given the same chance for existence, for earning a livelihood, for raising himself in the scales of manhood and womanhood, that are accorded to kindred nationalities.
>
> Treat him as a man; go into his home and learn of his social conditions; learn of his cares, his troubles and his hopes for the future; gain his confidence; open the doors of industry to him; let the word "Negro," "colored," and "black" be stricken from all the organizations enumerated in the federation of labor ... Obliterate race hatred, party prejudice, and help us to achieve nobler ends, greater results and become satisfactory citizens to our brother in white.
>
> This, Mr. Chairman, is perhaps the Negroes' temporary farewell to the American Congress; but let me say, phoenix-like he will rise up some day and come again. These parting words are in behalf of an outraged, heartbroken, bruised, and bleeding, but God-fearing people, faithful, industrious, loyal people-rising people, full of potential force.

After leaving Congress, White fled his native North Carolina for the North, fearful of political violence. He told the *Chicago Tribune*: "I cannot live in North Carolina and be a man and be treated as a man." White was the last southern black congressman for seventy years and the last from North Carolina until 1993. With his final speech in the House of Representatives in 1901, George White had, in effect, delivered the eulogy of the First Reconstruction.

Conclusion

This chapter was about democratic backsliding in the United States. Reconstruction shows that black officeholding alone was not a sufficient guarantee of multiracial democracy.

The 44th Congress, which met from 1875 to 1877, was the high point of black representation. It took nearly one hundred years for Congress to be as racially diverse again. Yet, the 44th Congress also coincided with the disastrous Compromise of 1877, which spelled the end of federal commitment to Reconstruction and left African Americans to the mercy of white racial terrorism in the South.[23] The survival of democracy in the United States, then, has little relationship to the electoral strength of racial minorities alone.

Multiracial democracy in the United States was undermined by unaccountable elites whose judicial attacks were not met with sufficient political challenge. The failure to disable the Supreme Court was perhaps the central shortcoming of the Reconstruction constitutional reforms. It was an opportunity missed once more during the Second Reconstruction. It is important to note that none of the Supreme Court's decisions ruled against the right of African Americans to vote directly. When the Supreme Court refused to strike down the literacy test and the grandfather clause,[24] it did so because there was no explicit racial content to them, even if it was obvious to everyone what their intended purpose was. Justice Joseph McKenna defended these devices in *Williams v. Mississippi* (1898) on the grounds that "they do not on their face discriminate between the races, and it has not been shown that their actual administration was evil; only that evil was possible under them."

Thus, Morgan Kousser (1984: 39) is right to point out that "never after the passage of the Fifteenth Amendment were all southern blacks disenfranchised." This is an important point. Middle-class blacks were sometimes able to pay the poll tax or pass the literacy test. The fact that some blacks were sometimes able to vote, however, does not make these devices non-racist. Total black disenfranchisement was never necessary for total white power. This lesson should be kept in mind as further facially non-racial measures are passed in states today making it harder for African Americans to vote.

The rise and fall of the First Reconstruction serve as a corrective to anyone enchanted by the triumphalist claims that the United States has undergone a clear process of ever-deepening democratization. In reality, democracy in the United States has been relatively short-lived, inconsistent, and underdeveloped.

3

The Rise of the Second Reconstruction

You see, Mississippi is not actually Mississippi's problem. Mississippi is America's problem. Because if America wanted to do something about what has been going on in Mississippi, it could have stopped by now.

Fannie Lou Hamer, *The Heritage of Slavery* (1968)

On July 25, 1946, two married couples were driving near Moore's Ford Bridge in Georgia. Their names were George and Mae Dorsey and Roger and Dorothy Malcolm. George Dorsey was a World War II veteran who had returned only nine months earlier after five years serving his country in North Africa and the Pacific. Dorothy Malcolm was seven months pregnant. Both couples were African American, and racial tensions in Georgia were running high.

The previous week, the Georgia Democratic Party had held primaries for state offices, including governor. For the first time since Reconstruction, thousands of African Americans had been allowed to vote. Before this point, state Democratic parties in the South had allowed only whites to vote in primary elections. Leaders argued that a party was a private organization and, therefore, membership eligibility was an organizational matter. Thanks to the Supreme Court's deconstructive ruling in the *Civil Rights Cases* of 1883, federal laws were deemed unable to prevent private organizations from discriminating on the basis of race. The violent suppression of the Republican and Populist parties at the end of the First Reconstruction had left the Democratic Party without any functioning opposition in the South. So nomination in a Democratic primary was tantamount to election, and the exclusion of African Americans like the Dorseys and the Malcolms from Democratic primaries effectively excluded them from electoral politics altogether.

By this point, however, the absurdity of calling the Democratic Party a private members' organization had become obvious. Two years earlier, the Supreme Court ruled in *Smith v. Allwright* (1944) that a formal prohibition on blacks voting in primaries violated the Fifteenth Amendment. This was a monumental decision, which Robert Mickey (2015) credits with being the starting gun of the process of democratizing the South. At first, Georgia refused to implement the *Smith v. Allwright* decision, but the NAACP successfully sued the state, and a federal court forced Georgia Democrats to hold an integrated primary on July 17, 1946.

The Crisis, the official magazine of the NAACP, recorded the Georgia decision as "an American revolution. It is probably the most important step toward erasing racial inequalities since Emancipation. It marks the beginning of a new day for the Negro, for the South, and for the nation."[1] One sign of these extraordinary developments was that the Department of Justice under President Harry Truman sent FBI agents to Georgia to investigate black voter suppression. Their presence, although light on the ground, made the July 1946 primaries the first time since Ulysses Grant that a presidential administration had made a serious effort to protect black voting rights (Mickey 2015: 126).

Black turnout was still highly suppressed as a result of legal challenges and threats of violence. When the leading gubernatorial candidate Eugene Talmadge was asked about the best way to keep blacks from voting, he replied with one word: "Pistols." On polling day, Talmadge supporters physically blocked African Americans from their polling stations, while Talmadge himself told police officers that, if they looked the other way, he would give them pay increases once elected. Talmadge won the election, described by the *New Republic* as "the most monstrous perversion of democracy imaginable."[2] In spite of this intimidation, about 85,000 black Georgians were able to vote (out of a total black population of about one million).

The Dorseys and Malcolms may have been among the African Americans who voted for the first time in their lives in that primary. Revenge came eight days later. On their drive down the quiet country road near Moore's Ford Bridge, a group of twenty white men stopped the Dorseys' car. The assailants led the occupants to the side of the road at gun point, tied the two couples (including the heavily pregnant Dorothy Malcolm) to a tree, and pumped sixty bullets into them.[3] No one was ever charged. George Dorsey fought fascism abroad only to die at the hands of white supremacists in the United States. As NAACP leader Moorfield Story bitterly commented, before the United States could "make the world safe for democracy," it needed first to "make America safe for Americans."[4]

* * *

The murders at Moore's Ford Bridge in 1946 tell us a couple of things about the rise of the Second Reconstruction. First, the Second Reconstruction required the Supreme Court to reverse the numerous anti-civil rights decisions which it had made over the previous decades. The court's decision in *Smith v. Allright* (1944) was significant because it was the first time since the 1860s that the court had opted for a more expansive interpretation of the Reconstruction amendments. After decades of excusing and facilitating the exclusion of African Americans from democratic participation, the court reconfirmed their basic citizenship rights.[5]

The second thing the murders reveal is that the re-democratization of the United States would take more than supportive Supreme Court rulings. The willingness of white supremacists to contest multiracial democracy through violence had not gone away. Expressions of black political power were met with brutality. Local officials were complicit in these actions, showing little willingness to prosecute perpetrators of racial violence and discrimination. Massive federal intervention, with a robust physical presence on the ground, was once more required to ensure that African Americans could exercise their citizenship rights freely.

This chapter is about the democratization of the United States in the second half of the twentieth century. It argues that, like with the First Reconstruction, the Second Reconstruction was largely made possible by a transformative set of legal reforms legislated by Congress and enforced by supportive presidential administrations, sometimes with military force. The political context that made these reforms possible was in large part creditable to sustained grassroots activism, international pressures, and mobilization of millions of ordinary African Americans, often in the face of violence.

This chapter differs from many other accounts of the civil rights era in that it de-emphasizes the positive role of the Supreme Court. There is no doubt that the Warren Court was an ally of democratization, and the NAACP pursued an important legal strategy (Francis 2014). But most of the "landmark" decisions of the court were simply undoing the court's earlier attacks (see Table 3.1). The federal judiciary should not get undue credit for simply clearing up its own mess. The Second Reconstruction was driven by democratic reforms that were largely achieved by political activists and implemented by elected officials. Sustained grassroots activism and moments of crisis put heavy pressure on these officials to act.

Table 3.1: Earlier Supreme Court decisions overturned during the Second Reconstruction

Judicial deconstruction	Year	Judicial reconstruction	Year	Content	Reconstruction amendment
Williams v. Mississippi	1898	South Carolina v. Katzenbach	1965	Discrimination in voter registration	Fifteenth
Civil Rights Case	1883	Heart of Atlanta Motel, Inc. v. US	1964	Racial segregation in places of public accommodation	Fourteenth
Pace v. Alabama	1883	Loving v. Virginia	1967	Interracial marriage	Fourteenth
Plessy v. Ferguson	1896	Irene Morgan v. Commonwealth of Virginia	1946	Segregation in inter-state travel	Fourteenth
Cumming v. Richmond County Board of Education	1899	Brown v. Board of Education	1954	School segregation	Fourteenth
Hodges v. United States	1906	Jones v. Alfred Mayer Co.	1968	Racial discrimination in private contracts	Thirteenth
Grovey v. Townsend	1935	Smith v. Allwright	1944	All-white primaries	Fifteenth
Breedlove v. Suttles	1937	Harper v. Virginia State Board of Elections	1966	Poll tax	Fifteenth
Colegrove v. Green	1946	Baker v. Carr	1962	Racial bias in legislative apportionment	Fifteenth

Executive Branch: Enforcing Constitutional Rights

In the years between the end of the First Reconstruction and the rise of the Second Reconstruction, the White House sat on its hands. Racial violence raged in the states. Thousands of African Americans were killed and maimed. Millions were denied equal citizenship. The United States existed in "a framework of contrived anarchy" (Kato 2015: 254). The basic function of the state, as Thomas Hobbes noted in *Leviathan* (1651), is to protect its citizens from wanton violence from others. The US government manifestly failed to do this, a clear demonstration of "racialized state failure" (Miller 2015).

Since the Compromise of 1877, various administrations – from Rutherford Hayes to Franklin Roosevelt – engaged in a mix of shameful inaction and active participation in racial discrimination. Even Franklin Roosevelt's New Deal and GI Bills embraced racist state rules, excluding the majority of African Americans from the rapid growth of the US welfare state.[6] When states discriminated against African Americans, the executive branch regularly cited Supreme Court decisions to justify their inaction. Roosevelt's Justice Department advised US attorneys that the Reconstruction amendments could not be used to prosecute individual civil rights violations. Writing in 1940, Assistant Attorney General John Rogge stated:

> The Constitution deals primarily with relationships between governmental authorities and between private people and authorities, rather than the relationships of private people to one another. Consequently ... vigilante or Ku Klux Klan activity, whether directed against reds, nazis, negroes, soap-box speakers, Jehovah's Witnesses, Jews or Catholics, is not within [federal authority].

Rogge cited the appalling *US v. Cruikshank* (1876) decision to justify his position, calling it "the earliest and leading case" on federal jurisdiction over private acts of racial violence.[7]

The political reaction to the Dorsey and Malcolm murders highlights key parallels in the paths of the two Reconstructions. In both Reconstructions, white acceptance of equal citizenship for blacks was partly predicated on their wartime sacrifice. More than 175,000 African Americans served in the Union army during the Civil War. This extraordinary figure represented nearly one in ten Union soldiers and double the number of eligible free black men of fighting age (15–40) living in the North.[8] Sympathetic images of noble black veterans filled the northern press, held up as models of republican liberty. It was this sacrifice that persuaded Abraham Lincoln to accept the idea of black voting in the final week of his life.

During World War II, more than 1.2 million African Americans served in the US armed forces. There was an irony in black soldiers fighting for freedom against race-based fascism in racially segregated units, but black leaders supported the war effort.[9] They promoted what they called a "Double V" strategy. Victory for freedom abroad would lead to victory for freedom at home. This strategy, deliberately mirroring the experience of the First Reconstruction, proved effective, but its success was not automatic. Initially, black veterans returned to southern states where they could not vote, and they were not able to use the GI Bill to attend their state's top universities or access veterans' housing in white neighborhoods.

Moments of crisis prompted forceful federalism for racial equality. Photographs of Dorsey's flag-draped coffin were plastered across American newspapers, echoing the images of brave black Union veterans with missing limbs. Mary Dudziak (2000) argues that the Dorsey/Malcolm murders were instrumental in pushing President Harry Truman to desegregate the US military. Truman's presidential report on civil rights ("To Secure These Rights") the following year explicitly stated that "the existence of discrimination against minority groups in the United States has an adverse effect upon our relations with other countries. Racial discrimination furnishes grist for the Communist propaganda mills."

Other incidents in the 1940s, 1950s, and 1960s – which civil rights groups ensured received media attention – drove further action from the federal government. In 1957, Secretary of State John Foster Dulles pleaded with Alabama governor James Folsom to halt the execution of a black handyman named Jimmy Wilson, who had been sentenced to death by an all-white jury for stealing $1.95 from an elderly white woman. Folsom relented due to the "international hullabaloo," and commuted Wilson's sentence to sixteen years in prison (Dudziak 2000: 6).

Early in the spring of 1961, an international incident nearly erupted when William Fitzjohn, Sierra Leone's first ambassador to the United States, was on his way to Pittsburgh for a lecture. The ambassador stopped for dinner with his driver at a Howard Johnson restaurant in rural Pennsylvania. Both men were refused service because of their race. In a damage limitation exercise, President John Kennedy invited Fitzjohn to the White House and he also arranged for the owner of the restaurant chain to deliver an apology. The mayor of the Pennsylvania town invited Fitzjohn to an elaborate dinner with the municipality's leading citizens.

As new nations emerged from colonialism in Africa, Asia, and Latin America, they faced a choice between the American and Soviet models (Maga 1992).[10] Images of lynched veterans, meek seamstresses arrested for riding the bus, and children pelted with missiles on the way to school became hugely inconvenient in the United States' Cold War strategy (Fraser 2000). Truman told Congress in early 1948: "If we wish to inspire the peoples of the world whose freedom is in jeopardy ... we must correct the remaining imperfections in our practice of democracy."[11]

Many in the Democratic Party recognized this imperative when the party gathered for its convention in Philadelphia in July 1948. At the convention, Minneapolis mayor Hubert Humphrey declared that there must be "no hedging – no watering down – of the instruments of the civil rights program." He memorably told the delegates that "the time has arrived for the Democratic Party to get out of the shadow of states' rights and walk forthrightly into the bright sunshine of human rights."[12] Humphrey's intervention was decisive in the convention's subsequent adoption (by 651.5 votes to 582.5 votes) of a civil rights program, for the first time in the Democratic Party's history. In turn, this vote led to the departure of thirty-five southern delegates from the convention and the formation of the States' Rights Democratic Party (the "Dixiecrats").

In addition to foreign policy concerns, the electoral incentives of the Democratic Party had changed. In the first half of the twentieth century, the savage violence of Jim Crow drove 7.5 million African Americans to flee from the South to the North. This movement of people, euphemistically called "The Great Migration," was the worst refugee crisis in American history. By 1970, only half of African Americans lived in the South – a dramatic change from the First Reconstruction, when about 90 percent of black people lived in the former Confederate states (see Figure 3.1).

Protected to a larger extent (although not completely) from the wanton violence that characterized their lives in the South, northern African Americans were better able to use their labor and vote to exercise political influence. Truman's decision to desegregate the armed forces the week after the 1948 convention showed that the national Democratic Party leadership had concluded – for the first time ever – that being outwardly pro-civil rights was to its electoral advantage. The Truman administration became the first to side voluntarily

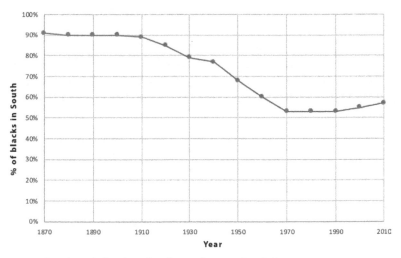

Note: South is defined as the eleven former Confederate states
Figure 3.1: Proportion of African Americans living in the South (1870–2010)

with civil rights plaintiffs in federal court since the First Reconstruction, filing supportive *amicus curiae* briefs in a variety of cases: *Shelley v. Kraemer* (1948), *Henderson v. US* (1949), *McLaurin v. Oklahoma State Regents* (1950), *Sweatt v. Painter* (1950), *Brown v. Board of Education* (1954).[13]

Truman's position on civil rights differed from that of his predecessor Franklin Roosevelt. New Deal social policies did little to counter segregation and, in many cases, entrenched and exacerbated material racial inequality (Katznelson 2013). The Roosevelt administration expanded segregation by implementing it in new divisions of the government, such as the Machine Records Branch and the Geological Survey Unit (King 1995). Roosevelt lost the black vote heavily in his first campaign, winning the support of only 23 percent of African Americans who could vote in 1932. Truman secured a higher share of the black vote in 1948 (77 percent) than Roosevelt did in any of his four elections, including his historic 1936 landslide. If Truman had not won such overwhelming support from African Americans in 1948, he would have lost Ohio, California, and Illinois – and, with them, the presidency (Sitkoff 1971). Even as late as the final year of Roosevelt's presidency, as many African Americans identified in surveys as Republicans as they did Democrats. The decisive switch in party identification did not occur until the Truman presidency (Bositis 2004: 9).

Humphrey's convention speech and Truman's desegregation order began the process by which the Democrats would transform into the party of civil rights, and, eventually, the Republicans would become a refuge of white supremacists. This was a lengthy process, which would take decades. The emotional ties voters feel to political parties, especially to those that generations of their family had supported, cannot be easily shaken. Many white supremacists could not simply join the "party of Lincoln" in the same way that many African Americans had been reluctant to "turn the portrait of Lincoln to the wall" even after the Republican Party had abandoned them. At first, many white supremacists turned to third parties or independents, such as Strom Thurmond in 1948 and George Wallace in 1968. Unwittingly, these independent candidates weakened the influence of white supremacists in both main parties and strengthened the hand of pro-civil rights leaders. When the Democrats and Republicans overlapped ideologically on civil rights the most in the 1950s–70s, party leaders ensured a bipartisan consensus for the democratizing legal reforms of the Second Reconstruction.

Executive branch commitment was real and, in many instances, effective. President Dwight Eisenhower famously sent US troops to ensure the desegregation of Little Rock Central High School in 1957. The comparisons with the First Reconstruction were easy to make: a Republican president using federal troops to enforce the rights of African Americans subjugated by a southern state government, just weeks after Congress had passed its first civil rights bill since 1875. Southern newspapers erupted in predictable fury. The *Selma Times-Journal* screamed that federal agents in the South were "constitutional rapists and racial renegades ... [a] new occupation by carpetbag troops."[14] The *Montgomery Advertiser* expressed its disgust at "the sight of federal troops taking over our schools, enforcing brotherly love and making pals and playmates of black and white at the point of the bayonet."[15] The newspaper removed the portrait of the president from the newsroom.

Equally, it is important not to overstate the level of executive branch commitment to the Second Reconstruction. With the Little Rock example aside, Eisenhower's record of enforcement was variable. In multiple school desegregation cases, the president was absent. In 1956, he allowed Governor Allan Shivers of Texas to block African American children from attending a hitherto white school in Mansfield (Bowes 2019). Eisenhower failed to send troops to Tennessee to protect black students at Clinton High School, which led to the school being bombed in 1958.

The 1960s was the zenith of executive branch enforcement of civil rights, but even in this decade the reforming Johnson administration pulled back from the most far-reaching proposals. In response to the urban riots and rebellions of the "long, hot summer" of 1967, Johnson commissioned the Kerner Commission Report on Civil Disorders to investigate the causes of urban unrest. The eleven-member commission was composed of a range of liberal moderate figures on civil rights. When Oklahoma senator Fred Harris was asked to serve on the commission, the president told him over the phone, "I want you to remember you're a Johnson man." Harris dutifully replied, "I'm your friend, Mr. President, and I won't forget it." Johnson shot back, "If you do, Fred, I'll take out my pocketknife and cut your peter off" (Harris 2008: 108).

The Kerner Commission went to American cities and conducted a range of interviews with people who had been involved in or affected by the riots. Kerner Commission member Edward Brooke, the first African American popularly elected to the US Senate, recalled meeting with the black power leader Rap Brown in Harlem as part of his investigations:

> I remember that well ... They stood up and said I was a part of the problem. The fact that I was in the Senate. I said, tell me why I'm the problem? They said, because you're there. You joined the white hierarchy or whatever. And then they proceeded to jump on me, but they couldn't jump on me on issues because I think my record so far as civil rights legislation is concerned is almost unparalleled.[16]

In spite of the tense initial meeting, Brooke sided with many of the concerns of the inner-city African Americans. He publicly declared: "In my view, the riots ... are neither communist inspired nor the result of an interstate conspiracy ... Hunger, bad housing, ill health, and a lack of work need no allies to create an atmosphere which breeds violence" (Thurber 2013: 240). Brooke's words were echoed in the commission's final report in March 1968:

> Segregation and poverty have created in the racial ghetto a destructive environment totally unknown to most white

Americans. What white Americans have never fully understood – but what the Negro can never forget – is that white
society is deeply implicated in the ghetto. White institutions
created it; white institutions maintain it; and white society
condones it.

The Kerner Commission's findings were electric, and 740,000
copies of the report were sold in eleven days. Johnson was
furious: he had expected the commission to produce a
much more muted report. Partly as a result of this personal
betrayal and in the context of extreme political difficulties
that he was facing over the Vietnam War, Johnson ignored
many of the commission's findings.

In the 1980s, the Reagan administration attempted to
refashion the civil rights agenda in a more conservative
direction. When signing the Martin Luther King federal
holiday bill into law, Reagan declared that "true justice must
be color-blind" and based on "individual merit." This was
a distortion of King's own position, who argued for racial
reparations, even in his famous "I Have a Dream" speech.
While King did speak of the ideal whereby his children would
be judged not by the color of their skin but by the content
of their character, he also declared that African Americans
had come "to cash a check"; redeeming "a promissory note"
marked "insufficient funds." King decried the isolation of
African Americans "on a lonely island of poverty in the
midst of a vast ocean of material prosperity."

This was a core tension in the Second Reconstruction,
not dissimilar to the policy failures of the First. While there
was political commitment to the enforcement of liberal
rights by US presidents, social and labor rights were more
contested. President George H. W. Bush was prepared to
veto the Civil Rights Bill of 1990, an employment bill, on
the basis of his opposition to perceived affirmative action.
Yet he nonetheless signed a bill strengthening laws against
race-based employment discrimination the following year.
Even Reagan could not blanch on voting rights enforcement.
He signed an extension to the Voting Rights Act in 1982,

which strengthened the contents of the law considerably. Civil rights lawyer Joseph Rauh told the *Washington Post*: "It was no compromise at all. We got everything we wanted." Rauh, counsel for the Leadership Conference on Civil Rights, described the legislation Reagan signed as "the perfect bill."[17]

The record of the executive branch during the Second Reconstruction is mixed, but there was a basic bipartisan commitment at the presidential level to a framework of multiracial democratic inclusion. This bipartisanship was not present during the First Reconstruction, and it is a key difference between the two Reconstructions. From Truman to Obama, no single presidential administration fully turned against the enforcement of civil rights. Enforcement was patchy and sometimes weak (Wolters 1996). Even presidents who are credited with being assertive on civil rights, like Lyndon Johnson, lost their nerve at various points. But, while the First Reconstruction only saw one administration with any sustained commitment to black civil rights (the Grant administration of 1869–77), the Second Reconstruction saw executive branch enforcement endure, in some form, for six decades – from 1946 until 2016.

Legislation: Re-Democratizing the Constitution

The Second Reconstruction was an effort to re-democratize the US Constitution. Two amendments were added to the US Constitution (see Table 3.2). Both were of less consequence than the three revolutionary amendments of 1865–70, but they nonetheless gave constitutional standing to further expansions of the franchise. The Twenty-Third Amendment (1961) gave the District of Columbia voting rights in presidential elections. In 1960 Washington, DC, was 54 percent black and would rise to 71 percent black by the end of the decade. In effect, the amendment gave several hundred thousand African Americans the ability to vote for president. The Twenty-Fourth Amendment (1964) banned the use of poll taxes (or any other non-payment of taxes) as a disqualification from voting. Poll taxes had been used in all the former Confederate states after the Civil War to deny blacks access to the polls and were still in use in nearly half of the former Confederacy by the time of the Twenty-Fourth Amendment's ratification.[18]

Table 3.2: Constitutional amendments during the Second Reconstruction

Amendment	Year	President	Content
Twenty-Third	1961	John Kennedy (D)	Residents of Washington, DC (a majority-black city) are entitled to vote for president
Twenty-Fourth	1964	Lyndon Johnson (D)	The poll tax is unconstitutional; voting cannot be denied on the basis of not paying taxes

More significantly, Congress passed half a dozen major statutes to revive the full force of the earlier Reconstruction amendments. The Supreme Court had rendered these amendments largely useless, striking down vital civil rights legislation of the 1860s and 1870s. Congress needed to pass new versions of the mid-nineteenth-century legislation to revive the amendments' impact (see Table 3.3).

These statutes breathed new life into the Reconstruction Amendments (see Table 3.4). The first – the Civil Rights Act of 1957 – was largely an administrative statute. It helped to ensure a bureaucratic foothold for civil rights enforcement in the executive branch. The law, which was the first civil rights legislation since 1875, created the Civil Rights Division (CRD) within the Department of Justice, itself a legacy of the First Reconstruction, having been created by the Enforcement Act of 1870. The CRD is tasked with the enforcement of all major civil rights laws. During the Obama Administration, the CRD had a staff of about seven hundred and an annual budget of $160 million. Barack Obama's attorney general Eric Holder described the CRD as the Department of Justice's "crown jewel."

The next statute, the Civil Rights Act of 1960, was the weakest of the five Civil Rights Acts. It affirmed the right of

Table 3.3: Statutes of the First and Second Reconstructions (paired by closest equivalents)

First Reconstruction	Year	Content	Second Reconstruction	Year	Content
Enforcement Act	1870	Created the Department of Justice	Civil Rights Act of 1957	1957	Created the Civil Rights Division in the Department of Justice
Civil Rights Act of 1866	1866	Affirmed black voting rights, allowed African Americans to sue if denied voting rights	Civil Rights Act of 1960	1960	Affirmed black voting rights, allowed African Americans to sue if denied voting rights
Civil Rights Act of 1875	1875	Ended segregation in places of public accommodation and public transport	Civil Rights Act of 1964	1964	Ended segregation in places of public accommodation and public transport
Southern Homestead Act	1866	Provided subsidized government land for ex-slaves	Fair Housing Act	1968	Outlawed discrimination in housing
Military Reconstruction Acts	1867	Sent federal government to register African Americans to vote, protect them physically, and ensure their voting rights	Voting Rights Act	1965	Sent federal government to register African Americans to vote, protect them physically, and ensure their voting rights
Ku Klux Klan Act	1871	Sent the federal government to infiltrate and arrest white supremacists	N/A	N/A	N/A
Freedmen's Bureau Act	1865	Federal agents empowered to negotiate contracts between black laborers and white employers	Civil Rights Act of 1991	1991	Protected victims of racial discrimination who sue their employer

Table 3.4: The Civil Rights Acts of the Second Reconstruction (1957–91)

Year	President	Policy area	Provisions
1957	Dwight Eisenhower (R)	Bureaucracy	Created the Civil Rights Division within the Justice Department and the Commission on Civil Rights
1960	Dwight Eisenhower (R)	Voting	Empowered courts to appoint "voting referees" to report on instances of voting rights infringement
1964	Lyndon Johnson (D)	Segregation	Prohibited racial segregation in places of "public accommodation," public facilities, services, and employment
1968	Lyndon Johnson (D)	Housing	Outlawed racial discrimination in the sale or renting of a house and in mortgage-lending practices
1991	George H. W. Bush (R)	Labor	Closed loop-holes (created by the Supreme Court) which allowed employers to discriminate if there was "business justification"

African Americans to vote and gave them legal entitlement to sue if they were victims of racial discrimination. The US attorney general was also empowered to file suits on their behalf, but this power proved "awkward and time-consuming" (Perry and Parent 1995: 5). Furthermore, it gave courts the ability to appoint "voting referees" – federal examiners – who could research and report on instances of racial discrimination in voting. While not a completely toothless act, its effect paled in comparison to the much more forceful Voting Rights Act of 1965, discussed in the next section.

The most important of the five Civil Rights Acts of the Second Reconstruction was that of 1964. The first stage of the bill left the Senate judiciary committee in October 1963, a month before the assassination of John F. Kennedy. As with Lincoln and the Thirteenth Amendment, the murdered president saw his legislation move through the early stages of passage but did not live to see the legislation fully enacted. Also in parallel with Lincoln, Kennedy's death probably helped to advance the cause of civil rights by adding political pressure to pass the legislation, which had been subjected to the longest filibuster to date in US history.

The Civil Rights Act of 1964 was in large part a revival of the Civil Rights Act of 1875, which had been struck down by the Supreme Court in the *Civil Rights Cases* of 1883. In the *Civil Rights Cases*, the court disingenuously asserted that "individual invasion of individual rights is not the subject matter of the [Fourteenth] Amendment." It took until the 1964 Civil Rights Act to challenge this deconstructive ruling. The Civil Rights Act of 1964 (like that of 1875) prohibited racial discrimination in places of public accommodation, such as theaters, restaurants, and hotels. Importantly, it also prohibited racial discrimination from any entity that received federal funding. The federal government used its huge fiscal advantage to compel states, localities, and private organizations to integrate, lest they lose funding. When the Supreme Court tried to weaken enforcement of this power in *Grove City College v. Bell* (1984), Congress overturned the deconstructive judicial decision with the Civil Rights Restoration Act of 1987.

The first three Civil Rights Acts largely dealt with liberal rights and access to the public services. Yet, by the mid-twentieth century, Jim Crow segregation had exacerbated huge material inequalities. Residential segregation was worse at the start of the Second Reconstruction than it had been after the Civil War. In the 1860s, about 30 percent of urban African Americans lived in overwhelmingly black neighborhoods. Fifty years later, that proportion had increased to 40 percent. By the 1940s, after the first wave of African Americans moved north during the Great Migration, nearly 80 percent of black city-dwellers lived in almost entirely black neighborhoods (Klinkner and Smith 1999: 116).

In 1966, Lyndon Johnson tried to pass a bill to reduce residential segregation, but it was defeated by an unsympathetic Congress. After a long delay, the next session of Congress finally managed to push forward with a second attempt at passage in early 1968. On April 1, 1968, the liberal Republican senator Edward Brooke wrote to his former Boston University fraternity brother Martin Luther King to inform him of the bill's progress.[19] Writing "Dear Martin," Brooke thanked the civil rights leader for his "good and thoughtful telegrams supporting the current civil rights bill." He added, "I am greatly heartened by our success in obtaining Senate approval of the very substantial fair housing bill," but he noted that it would still take time to push the legislation through the House of Representatives. Brooke closed the letter, "I look forward to seeing you soon."[20] Three days later, Martin Luther King was shot dead outside his hotel room in Memphis, Tennessee. He was only 39 years old. King's death hastened the passage of the key civil rights bill. The Civil Rights Act of 1968, more popularly known as the Fair Housing Act, received House agreement within a week of King's death. The following day, on April 11, 1968, Lyndon Johnson signed the bill into law. It was a bittersweet moment for the bereft Edward Brooke, who stood next to the president at the signing ceremony.

In spite of coming more than two decades later than the earlier civil rights bills, it is worth including the Civil Rights Act of 1991 in the legislative history of the Second Reconstruction. During the First Reconstruction, numerous state legislatures passed laws to support the labor rights of African Americans, as was discussed in Chapter 1. At the federal level, the Freedmen's Bureau Act contained provisions to protect ex-slaves from exploitation in the labor market. President Andrew Johnson denounced the legislation as "an immense patronage," warning that the financial support would injure the "character" of the former slaves and lead to a "life of indolence." He instructed Congress that it ought to consider first "our own people."

Similar rhetoric occurred in the early 1990s as Congress moved to pass a piece of civil rights legislation focused on racial minorities' rights in the workplace. Half a dozen

Supreme Court decisions in the 1980s had weakened protections in the Civil Rights Act of 1964 by allowing employers to discriminate against workers on the basis of race if they could produce a business justification. In response, Congress voted overwhelmingly for the Civil Rights Act of 1990, which was designed to overturn all these deconstructive rulings. The legislation allowed employees to use an effect-based standard of racial discrimination in employment cases. The bill received the support of 65 percent of senators and 63 percent of representatives.

Opponents of the legislation, however, argued that it would lead to "racial quotas" in the workplace. The legislation was not designed as an "affirmative action" law, but it was on this basis that George H. W. Bush vetoed the law on October 22, 1990. In his veto statement, Bush warned: "The bill actually employs a maze of highly legalistic language to introduce the destructive force of quotas into our Nation's employment system." Two days later, Congress attempted to override the veto, but its efforts failed by one vote.

One of the leading opponents of the 1990 Civil Rights Bill was North Carolina Senator Jesse Helms, who was at the time engaged in a fierce election battle against Harvey Gantt, the former mayor of Charlotte. Gantt was the first black person ever to be nominated by the Democratic Party in any state to run for the US Senate. Helms told voters in North Carolina that the Civil Rights Bill "would have meant that nobody – nobody – would have been safe about a job or a promotion. It would be determined by race."[21] In the final week of the election, the Helms campaign unleashed a storm of negative advertisements about the Civil Rights Bill of 1990. In one, Helms conflated the bill with federal efforts to integrate schools, which he also opposed. He spoke to camera:

For twenty years, the Washington liberals have controlled education. Twenty years of mistakes: forced busing, neighborhood schools wrecked, plummeting SAT scores. And now comes Ted Kennedy's quota bill hiring teachers based on racial quotas and not qualifications. Mr. Gantt complains that I voted against federal controls of our schools – and you bet I did.

A second advert was undoubtedly the most famous of the campaign and, indeed, one of the most famous in US election history. The so-called "White Hands" advert, broadcast six days before the election, featured the hands of a white man who angrily crumples up a letter from a potential employer. The narrator explained:

> You needed that job. You were the best qualified, but they had to give it to a minority because of a racial quota. Is that really fair? Harvey Gantt says it is. Gantt supports Ted Kennedy's racial quota law that makes the color of your skin more important than your qualifications. You'll vote on this issue next Tuesday. For racial quotas: Harvey Gantt. Against racial quotas: Jesse Helms.

The advert alluded to concerns about job competition at a time when many blue-collar jobs in the state were disappearing. Gantt reflected in an interview that "we had been losing textile jobs in North Carolina, but they didn't have anything to do with affirmative action programs at all, but he paired ... the loss of jobs going overseas or other places with people's fear of affirmative action. And when you put those two combinations together, it becomes a dynamite ad."[22] Letetia Daniels Jackson, a Gantt campaign worker, agreed: "I think that it was clearly designed to scare white people in North Carolina who may have been excited by the campaign and may have felt that Harvey Gantt was a good candidate to basically say to them, *You better be careful because they're going to take your jobs. First they're going to take your Senate seat and then they're going to take your jobs.* It was that underlying racism."[23] A Gantt campaign worker recalled the vitriol that flowed from the advertisement while he was campaigning for Gantt in Sylva, North Carolina: "I'm 23 years old. I'm a white male. A guy walks up to me on the street. He says, 'Are you working for the Harvey Gantt campaign?' I said, 'Yes, I am.' And then, he spit on me. He said, 'I've seen that ad about Harvey Gantt taking jobs from white people.' I was really taken aback by it."[24] Harvey Gantt lost to Jesse Helms, 47 percent to 53 percent.

After the election, in the new session of Congress, a revised version of the 1990 bill was introduced. This version of the law made minor changes to the language of the earlier legislation and placed a cap on the amount of compensation civil rights litigants could be awarded. Jesse Helms was one of only five senators to vote against the legislation, which was signed into law by President George H. W. Bush in November 1991, just over a year after Gantt's historic defeat. At a ceremony in the Rose Garden, Bush declared: "Discrimination, whether on the base of race, national origin, sex, religion or disability is worse than wrong. It's an evil that strikes at the very heart of the American ideal. This bill, building on current law, will help ensure that no American will discriminate against another."

The Quiet Revolution in Voting Rights

The most important democratizing statute in US history is the Voting Rights Act of 1965. It is the centerpiece of the Second Reconstruction. When Lyndon Johnson signed the bill into law on August 6, 1965, he called it "a triumph for freedom as huge as any victory that has ever been won on any battlefield."[25] At his last press conference in January 1969, Johnson stated that he regarded the Voting Rights Act as his greatest achievement. His words echoed those of Ulysses Grant, who in 1870 declared that "the fifteenth amendment to the Constitution completes the greatest civil change and constitutes the most important event that has occurred since the nation came into life."[26] The Voting Rights Act brought the Fifteenth Amendment into full implementation.

There are three key features that stand out in their significance (see Table 3.5). First, Section 2 of the Act gave ordinary voters legal standing to sue any jurisdiction for voting rights violations. Second, Section 5 required states and municipalities with a history of minority voter suppression to seek approval from the federal government for even the slightest change to electoral law or practice. Third, Section 6 authorized the federal government to have a physical presence in these jurisdictions, which were mostly in the South. For the first time since the First Reconstruction, large numbers of federal agents were in the South to monitor elections, register African Americans to vote, and protect them at the ballot box.

Table 3.5: Summary of the Voting Rights Act of 1965

Section	Provision
Section 2	Enables American citizens to sue any jurisdiction or individual for any attempt to hinder their right to vote on the basis of race
Section 3	Attorney general may appoint federal examiners to oversee election disputes
Section 4	Formula for determining preclearance eligibility
Section 5	Federal preclearance (i.e., Justice Department or DC Circuit Court must approve any changes to electoral practice or law in any jurisdiction under Section 4)
Sections 6–8	Attorney general may send federal agents to register voters and monitor elections in any jurisdiction under Section 4
Section 9	Federal government has jurisdiction in all voting rights lawsuits
Section 10	Abolishes the poll tax
Section 11–14	Details of penalties for voting fraud
Sections 15–19	Miscellanea: funds, guarantees of existing rights, court strategy

The most coercive elements of the law were Sections 5 and 6. They deserve detailed attention because they stand out from other US civil rights statutes. Most civil rights laws in the United States, including the aforementioned Civil Rights Acts, have been premised on the expectation that victims of discrimination will sue for their equality in federal court. This can be a lengthy and costly process, which might deter some victims of racial discrimination. The Voting Rights Act was written from a different perspective. Using a formula in Section 4 of the Act, Congress identified areas of the country that had consistently shown resistance to equal citizenship for non-whites. It then gave the federal government (specifically, the Civil Rights Division in the Department of Justice) legal powers to overrule local officials and place a physical presence in the South. In effect, the Voting Rights Act placed the burden of proving non-discrimination on the historic perpetrators of discrimination rather than requiring victims of discrimination to seek remediation. In *South Carolina v. Katzenbach* (1966), confirming the constitutionality of the Voting Rights Act, Chief Justice Earl Warren concluded: "After enduring nearly a century of systematic resistance to the Fifteenth Amendment, Congress might well decide to shift the advantage of time and inertia from the perpetrators of the evil to its victims."

To avoid accusations that Congress was arbitrarily targeting the South, a formula based on historical voting data was used to determine eligibility. Originally, Section 4 covered all jurisdictions where fewer than 50 percent of the eligible voting population were on the voting rolls in the 1964 presidential election, or where a literacy test had been in place at the time of the ratification of the Twenty-Fourth Amendment. Later, under the bill's renewals in 1972, 1975, and 1982 (but not in the 2006 renewal), the formula was modified to take account of voting behavior through elections in the 1970s. While the Section 4 formula included jurisdictions that clearly required federal monitoring, such as all of the Deep South, it was criticized for key omissions (e.g., Florida, Ohio) and the inclusion of jurisdictions with very few minority voters (e.g., counties in Maine and Colorado). According to Howard Glickman, who worked in the Appeals and Research Section of the Civil Rights Division and helped to draft the bill: "We knew where the problems were – what states had to be covered – but you couldn't just name the state in the legislation" (Berman 2015: 32). The Section 4 formula, therefore, served as a pragmatic yet imperfect means to protect the voting rights of blacks and other ethnic minorities. In spite of not being modified in the Voting Rights Act's last renewal in 2006, Morgan Kousser has shown that the formula adopted in the 1982 renewal has remained a remarkably accurate predictor of where voting rights violations are likely to be (Kousser 2015). Congress extensively reviewed the evidence for changing Section 4 in 2006 and concluded that it was not necessary to do so.

Section 6 entailed the physical presence of federal agents in areas under the Section 4 formula. Direct comparisons were drawn by southerners to the First Reconstruction. The *Montgomery Advertiser* lamented in March 1965 that "it is about certain that President Johnson's reconstruction bill will be enacted."[27] In a memo written shortly before Johnson delivered his "We Shall Overcome" speech to Congress in March 1965, his long-time aide and fellow Texan Horace "Buzz" Busby warned that "to southern minds and mores ... the proposals of this message would represent a return to Reconstruction" (Berman 2015: 15). Busby's warning was prescient. Shortly after Johnson signed the act into law, the *Montgomery Advertiser* declared Alabama would be under "federal occupation," editorializing that "federal agents, lineal descendants of Reconstruction corrupters, will be at work showing illiterates where to make their marks."[28]

Between 1966 and 1974, the Justice Department sent 7,359 election observers to the South. Jimmy Carter sent about 3,000 federal agents to monitor elections in his one-term presidency alone. These agents were not simply passive observers. They actively sought out African Americans so as to register them to vote. One can only image the psychological difference Section 6 produced. For the first time since the First Reconstruction, agents from the government went to African Americans and *encouraged* them, rather than deterred them, to participate in electoral democracy. During the Johnson administration (1965–9), federal agents directly signed up 158,384 African Americans on the electoral rolls.

For decades prior to the Voting Rights Act, black voters had been forced to go to sometimes far-flung administrative buildings to plead with often unsympathetic local registrars to be placed on the electoral register. They were met with poll taxes, literacy tests, good character clauses, and residency requirements designed to block them from registering. Literacy tests asked applicants to recall sections of the Constitution verbatim, interpret complicated statutes, or produce obscure information, such as the names of state court judges.

The laws were written with sufficient flexibility as to empower local administrators – who were almost always white Democrats – to have the discretion to find loopholes for "deserving" applicants (whites) while denying registration to African Americans. While the grounds were spurious, the challenged voters were forced to go to court to clear their name, a burden that was simply too high a price to pay for many of the state's impoverished African Americans. Under the Voting Rights Act, the dynamic changed. The act made all of these devices illegal.

The Voting Rights Act ensured nationalized voting administration insofar as it was possible. Its standout feature was the Section 5 requirement that jurisdictions, identified under the Section 4 formula, with a history of voting rights violations seek approval from the federal government before bringing any changes in election law or practice. Jurisdictions under preclearance were forced to submit even the most minor changes for review by the Justice Department or the US District Court for the District of Columbia Circuit. It was a game changer against attempts by municipal and state legislatures to dilute the voting power of newly enfranchised African Americans.

Between 1965 and 2013, Section 5 was used to block more than three thousand electoral changes deemed by the federal government to be discriminatory (Berman 2015). A report from the National Commission on Voting Rights reveals that preclearance was overwhelmingly used to protect African Americans' voting rights. Between 1995 and 2013, 89.3

percent preclearance interventions protected black voters specifically (National Commission on Voting Rights 2014).

Within six years of the Voting Rights Act's passage, black voter registration had increased nearly 30 percentage points across Alabama, Georgia, Louisiana, Mississippi, North Carolina, South Carolina, and Virginia. According to David Garrow (1978: 19, 200), the suspension of literacy tests alone led to the enfranchisement of one million African Americans within five years. Black registration levels and black officeholding approached, although in many cases did not reach, levels proportionate to the First Reconstruction. In 1990, there were still fewer black state legislators in the South than there were in 1870; but by the start of the twentieth-first century, the region had finally caught up.

Many of the provisions of the Voting Rights Act, including Section 5's "preclearance," were written with an expiration date, forcing the law to be renewed by Congress four times. In each instance, the act was extended under a Republican president (Nixon, Ford, Reagan, Bush II); however, the partisan composition of Congress differed. In 1970 and 1975, both chambers of Congress were under Democratic control. In 1982, the House was controlled by the Democrats, while the Senate was in Republican hands. In 2006, the Voting Rights Act was renewed at a time when Republicans enjoyed unified control across all branches of the federal government. Each time the law has been renewed, it has been strengthened in some form.

Each of the debates over the renewal of the Voting Rights Act is informative for political scientists and historians in a variety of ways. Most obviously, they provide insight into public discourse about race at various junctures in recent American political development. Relatedly, they demonstrate the political strength of the memory of the civil rights movement, as well as the ways in which subsequent political actors have rendered its history for contemporary political purposes. The Voting Rights Act extension debates have highlighted the role of individual political actors in the survival or demise of particular legislation, and the act has attracted unlikely allies in Congress, such as the conservative congressmen Henry Hyde (R-IL), Jim Sensenbrenner (R-WI), Bo Ginn (D-GA), and Senator Bob Dole (R-KS) (May 2013: Ch 8; Berman 2015).

In the first two decades of universal African American voting rights, nearly all black office-seekers were elected in areas where African Americans formed a majority of voters. There were a couple of notable exceptions – the Republican senator Edward Brooke in Massachusetts and the socialist Democratic congressman Ron Dellums in Berkeley, California – but the vast majority of black elected officials were elected in jurisdictions where their victory was possible without winning a single white vote (Cutler 1972; Cannon 1999; Brooke 2007; Rigueur 2015; Johnson 2018).

In the 1980s, however, signs of success were apparent in some majority white jurisdictions. African American Alan Wheat was elected to Congress in 1982 to represent the predominantly white liberal Fifth District of Missouri. His predecessor Richard Bolling, a white Democrat, had been instrumental in ensuring the passage of the 1957 Civil Rights Act. He introduced the discharge petition which released the Civil Rights Act of 1964 from the Senate, a crucial move in the bill's passage. Also, in 1982, another African American, Los Angeles mayor Tom Bradley, came agonizingly close to being elected governor of California (Pettigrew and Alston 1988). Soon after, Harvey Gantt was elected mayor of Charlotte, North Carolina, becoming the first black mayor of a predominantly white southern city in the twentieth century. Yet, even as Jesse Jackson sought the presidency for a second time in 1988, still no African American had been elected governor of any state.[29]

This hurdle was cleared two days before the Berlin Wall came down. On November 7, 1989, voters in the state of Virginia – the former capital of the Confederacy – elected L. Douglas Wilder, the grandson of slaves, as their governor. In the years that followed, African Americans were elected to major offices in a variety of majority white jurisdictions. The pinnacle of this achievement occurred nineteen years after the Wilder victory, when Barack Hussein Obama was elected president of the United States.

No state, since the nineteenth century, has been majority African American, and therefore all major political offices in the United States – senator, governor, and president – require African Americans to be elected in contexts in which they are not in the majority. The capacity of African Americans to secure white support for this level of elections, then, is intimately linked with claims about the vitality of democratic inclusion in the United States. If democracy entails access to all levels of power for all members of that society, then the election of African Americans to these major offices must be understood as a feature of American democratization.

Conclusion

The United States' experience with multiracial democracy is remarkably short. Most African Americans have been able to exercise the right to vote only since the 1960s. With the brief exception of the First Reconstruction, essential features of a democratic polity were not available to millions of US residents until the mid-twentieth century. Göran Therborn was correct when he argued in 1977 that the United States was one of the *last* major industrialized nations to democratize, not one of the first. It was not until the passage of the Voting Rights Act in 1965 that African Americans began to win elected offices in substantial numbers. Black officeholding was dependent on the massive intervention of the federal government, secured through legislative reforms, judicial interventions, constitutional amendments, and the physical presence of federal agents monitoring the voting rights of African Americans. These developments transformed American democracy, producing a "quiet revolution" in voting rights (McDonald 1989; Davidson and Grofman 1994).

Multiracial democratization in the United States has only ever been possible when the national government has used its full coercive powers to protect, physically and legally, the equal citizenship of racial minorities. Democracy has to be fought for constantly – any letting up allows the anti-democratic forces of white supremacy to re-emerge. Martin Luther King's attorney J. L. Chestnut reflected: "Almost every step of progress for black people required either confrontation – a lawsuit, a boycott, a march, or the threat of them – or a federal regulation requiring black partici-pation as a condition for receiving money" (2007: 268).

4

The Compromise of 2016

It is called perpetuation of racial entitlement. It's been written about. Whenever a society adopts racial entitlements, it is very difficult to get out of them through the normal political processes. I don't think there is anything to be gained by any senator to vote against continuation of this act. And I am fairly confident it will be re-enacted in perpetuity unless – unless a court can say it does not comport with the Constitution.

Justice Antonin Scalia, oral arguments in
Shelby County v. Holder (2013)

Two years into his first term, things looked bleak for Barack Obama. In the 2010 midterm elections, Democrats suffered their worst defeats at the congressional level since 1938. Republicans gained six governorships. Twenty legislative chambers flipped from Democratic to Republican control. Hundreds of Democratic state legislators lost their seats. The Republicans gained more state legislative districts off the Democrats that year than the Democrats had gained off the Republicans in the wake of Watergate.[1] The political backlash against the election of the first black president was prodigious.

The political convulsion was most clearly felt in Alabama. For the first time since the 1870s, Republicans gained control of the Alabama state legislature. During the First Reconstruction, Republicans passed civil rights statutes guaranteeing "equal civil and political rights and public privileges" and established a universal public school system. So committed to equal citizenship were the Alabama Republicans that they made it a constitutional requirement that every voter in the state take the following oath: "I accept the civil and political equality of all men; and agree not to attempt to deprive any person or persons, on account of race, color, or previous condition, of any political or civil right, privilege, or immunity, enjoyed by any other class of men."

With this record, it is unsurprising that the vast majority of Alabama's African American population voted for the Republicans in the nineteenth century. Most whites voted Democrat. It was in the interests of the Democratic Party to keep African Americans from voting. The fewer black voters there were, the fewer Republican voters there would be. To achieve this end, Democrats introduced a range of legal devices that made it harder for African Americans to register to vote, cast their ballots, and vote in competitive electoral districts. The Democrats were so successful in their efforts that they effectively destroyed the Republican Party in Alabama for a century.

John Knox, the president of the Alabama constitutional convention that ratified the state's racist post-Reconstruction constitution in 1901, argued in favor of a literacy test to ensure that "[t]he negro is not discriminated against on account of his race but on account of his intellectual and moral condition." Pointing to the fact that other restrictions, such as property requirements, were declared constitutional by the judiciary, Knox argued that a literacy test could be justified on a similar color-blind basis. He explained:

> If it be said that this exception permits many more white people to vote than negroes, the answer was that this would be equally true of any proper qualification which might be proposed. It would be true of an educational qualification,

and it would be true of a property qualification, the validity of which has never been questioned.[2]

As late as 1959, the Supreme Court supported the notion that such restrictions, which we now regard as incontrovertibly racist, were race-neutral. In *Lassiter v. Northampton County Board of Elections*, the much-lionized Warren Court ruled that if literacy tests were applied to everyone, then they could not be racially discriminatory and were, therefore, constitutional. In the court's opinion, Justice William Douglas explained, "[l]iteracy and illiteracy are neutral on race, creed, color, and sex ... [I]n our society where newspapers, periodicals, books, and other printed matter canvass and debate campaign issues, a State might conclude that only those who are literate should exercise the franchise."

It took the Voting Rights Act of 1965, signed by a Democratic president, to bring such practices to an end. By this point, the Democratic Party was the growing home of Alabama African Americans, while white Alabamans defected to the Republican Party. A time-traveler from the 1870s would be bemused to find that Alabama politics today is once more characterized by stark racially polarized partisanship, but the party roles are reversed. In the 2008 election, only 2 percent of African Americans in Alabama voted Republican, while only 10 percent of whites voted Democratic. For Republicans, who represent the state's white majority, this racially polarized partisanship is to their electoral advantage. As the chair of the Alabama Democratic Party reflected after the 2010 elections, "the Alabama Republican Party wants it so that whenever you see a person with a 'D' next to his or her name on TV, that person is black."[3]

In those elections, white voters in Alabama's Shelby County made a final and definitive switch to the Republican Party. They dumped incumbent Democratic state representative Jimmy Martin in favor of Republican Kurt Wallace. As election day approached, Martin could see the writing on the wall for his doomed campaign. Turning to his wife Norma, he said, "I think we've got another Goldwater sweep coming through," a reference to the 1964 presidential election between Republican Barry Goldwater and Democrat Lyndon Johnson. That year, Alabamans abandoned the Democratic Party at the federal level to support Goldwater, who had voted against the Civil Rights Act of 1964. Not everyone in the Republican Party was thrilled by Goldwater's success among anti-civil rights whites. The black Republican Edward Brooke, whose grandfather had been a slave, lamented that his party's success in the Deep South that year was "an exception which is more cause for alarm than satisfaction" (Brooke 1966: 7).

The "Goldwater sweep" of 2010 was the final expression of the decades-long process of white flight from the Democratic Party. Fred Barnes celebrated in the *Weekly Standard*: "To say the politics of Alabama have changed doesn't quite capture it. The wildest dreams of Republicans have come true. They won everything in the November 2 elections: all statewide offices from top to bottom, both houses of the legislature for the first time in 136 years."[4] Such victories were replicated across the country, especially in the South and Midwest. With their new-found power, Republican state legislatures and local governments soon went about passing laws that had long been blocked by Democrats, such as policies that made it easier for school districts to avoid racial integration orders (Johnson and King 2019).

One area in which Republicans were thwarted from achieving policy change was in electoral law. Due to Section 5 of the Voting Rights Act, many southern jurisdictions were required to seek approval from the Obama administration for the smallest change to election law or practice. From the perspective of Republicans who had won such commanding majorities, this requirement was indefensible and humiliating. Shelby County sued the Justice Department in federal court. The county hired Bert Rein, an experienced lawyer, to represent them. In the 1960s, Rein had been a clerk for Justice John Harlan, a vocal opponent of the expansion of voting rights. The year Rein served as his clerk, Justice

Harlan dissented in the case *Harper v. Virginia State Board of Elections* (1966), which found the poll tax to be unconstitutional. Harlan, echoing the anti-Reconstruction justices of the nineteenth century, pronounced: "neither does the Equal Protection Clause of that Amendment [the Fourteenth] rigidly impose upon America an ideology of unrestrained egalitarianism."

The case *Shelby County, Alabama v. Attorney General Eric Holder* was taken to the US District Court for the District of Columbia. On behalf of Shelby County, Rein argued: "[I]t is no longer constitutionally justifiable for Congress to arbitrarily impose on Shelby County and other covered jurisdictions disfavored treatment by forcing them to justify all voting changes to federal officials in Washington, DC." District Court Judge John Bates disagreed. Bates described Section 5's re-adoption in the 2006 renewal of the Voting Rights Act as "carefully considered" and "the protections of Section 5 were still needed to safeguard racial and language minority voters." He threw out Shelby County's complaint.

Shelby County did not accept defeat. In May 2012, the case was heard by US Court of Appeals for the DC Circuit. Once more, Rein and his Shelby County clients were unsuccessful. The presiding judge, David Tatel, who succeeded Ruth Bader Ginsberg on the Court of Appeals in 1994, wrote: "After thoroughly scrutinizing the record and given that overt racial discrimination persists in covered jurisdictions notwithstanding decades of section 5 preclearance, we, like the district court, are satisfied that Congress's judgment deserves judicial deference." The Voting Rights Act had won another victory.

Six months later, on November 6, 2012, Barack Obama was re-elected president of the United States. Obama's re-election was, in some ways, more remarkable than his first. African American turnout exceeded white turnout for the first time since Ulysses Grant's re-election in 1872. Increased participation from non-white voters was crucial, because Obama's support among white voters had declined since 2008. In fact, Barack Obama was elected in 2012 with the lowest share of the white two-party vote of any president in US history. African American voters had saved the first black presidency from an early end.

The victorious glow of Obama's re-election was soon snuffed out. Three days later, the Supreme Court issued a writ of *certiorari* for *Shelby County v. Holder*. About ten thousand circuit court cases are appealed to the Supreme Court each year, but the nine justices only have time to hear about eighty-five of them. A writ of *certiorari* is the court's way of declaring which cases it wants to hear. If the justices take no action, then the lower court ruling stands. In the writ of November 9, 2012, the Supreme Court stated that it wanted to consider, "[w]hether Congress' decision in 2006 to reauthorize Section 5 of the Voting Rights Act under the pre-existing coverage formula of Section 4(b) of the Voting Rights Act exceeded its authority under the Fourteenth and Fifteenth Amendments and thus violated the Tenth Amendment and Article IV of the United States Constitution." In less technical language, the court wanted to decide whether federal preclearance remained constitutional.

When the case was heard in February 2013, the reaction of the justices was not encouraging. Justice Antonin Scalia interrupted oral argument to enter into a lengthy discourse about "racial entitlements." Scalia argued that the survival of the Voting Rights Act was "very likely attributable, to a phenomenon that is called perpetuation of racial entitlement." Scalia implied that Section 5 gave special privileges to non-whites unfairly. Because of the act's prestige, Scalia posited, no politician would be brave enough to repeal it. He opined sarcastically: "Even the name of it is wonderful: The Voting Rights Act. Who is going to vote against that in the future?" He predicted, "it will be re-enacted in perpetuity unless ..." He slightly stuttered, perhaps pausing to consider how much of his hand he should reveal. He continued, "unless a court can say it does not comport with the Constitution."

Four months later, in a 5–4 decision, the Supreme Court

quashed Section 5 of the Voting Rights Act by arguing that the preclearance formula in Section 4 adopted by Congress in 2006 unfairly punished some parts of the country for past wrongs that had since been remedied. The consequence of this decision was to give jurisdictions with histories of severe racial discrimination power to change election law and practices, which they had not been free to do since the 1960s. Just over three years later, Donald Trump was elected president.

* * *

In *The Two Reconstructions* (2004), Richard Valelly made the important point that those who lived during the First Reconstruction did not know that it would fail totally. Indeed, it might have seemed absurd to suggest in the 1870s that a country with hundreds of black elected officials would have none thirty years later. It surely would have been seen as excessive pessimism to suggest that the state constitutions and federal statutes guaranteeing the right to vote, equality under the law, and universal education would all be repealed. It would have been hard to imagine that federal judges would willingly misinterpret the Constitution to deprive Americans of their basic rights as citizens. Yet, all of this occurred between 1876 and 1901 – one generation.

Valelly's insight is a useful corrective to ideas of historical inevitability. Those living in a particular historical moment have no idea how it is going to end. But Valelly did not apply the same insight to the Second Reconstruction. He wrote: "We now have a fairly firm sense that the second reconstruction is irreversible" (2004: 20). This view now appears much too sanguine. Even in 2004, Valelly's words were difficult to maintain. The key undemocratic institution within the US Constitution – the Supreme Court – had been steadily dismantling the legal infrastructure of the Second Reconstruction since the 1970s. Valelly listed a number of key cases that had weakened the Voting Rights Act and, by implication, black voting rights: *Mobile v. Bolden* (1980), *Shaw v. Reno* (1993), *Miller v. Johnson* (1995), *Reno v. Bossier Parish* (2000). But he then added, "whether these changes have actually harmed black enfranchisement is not obvious" (2004: 237). It is obvious now.

This chapter analyzes the forces that are unraveling the United States' second experiment with multiracial democracy. The end of the First Reconstruction is typically identified as the 1876 election, when the popular-vote loser Rutherford Hayes was installed in the presidency by the electoral college on the understanding that he would withdraw federal troops from the South and return the southern states to "home rule." While Hayes's election is significant, excessive focus on it renders an incomplete understanding of how the First Reconstruction was dismantled and by whom. By the time Hayes became president, the Supreme Court had already begun its devastating crusade against the Reconstruction statutes and amendments. The *Slaughterhouse Cases* were decided four years before Hayes became president. Congress fell to anti-Reconstruction forces two years before Hayes's election. Judicial attack and racially polarized partisanship predated the Compromise of 1877.

Black voting rights did not come to an immediate end after 1876. As I showed in Chapter 2, efforts at multiracial democracy persisted, often in the face of extreme political violence, for another generation. In the 1890s, coalitions of black Republicans and white Populists achieved some success at state and local levels. There was even an attempt to protect black voting rights in Congress in 1890. Reconstruction did not come fully to an end until the start of the twentieth century, when the Reconstruction state constitutions were torn up by state constitutional conventions that excluded Republicans from participation.

This chapter's title is an allusion to the Compromise of 1877 with this wider historical context in mind. Rutherford Hayes and Donald Trump were not similar men. Hayes was a war hero, a lawyer who defended runaway slaves, and a reformer. He was eulogized as "an industrious and conscientious civil officer, a soldier of dauntless courage, a loyal comrade and friend, a sympathetic and helpful neighbor, and the honored head of a happy Christian home."[5] Donald Trump avoided service in the Vietnam War, inherited his business from his father who was prosecuted for violating the Fair Housing Act, and has done little to "drain the swamp" of monied influence. Trump's eulogy is unlikely to sound similar to the one President Benjamin Harrison delivered for Hayes in 1893.

In spite of their many differences, the men share some similarities. They were both Republicans, elected on the heels of two historic elections in which African Americans played a decisive role. Their predecessors' terms had both seen a rise of racially polarized partisanship partly as backlash against their pro-civil rights stance. Civil rights had been attacked by the Supreme Court before either Hayes or Trump arrived in office, and the judicial onslaught continued during their presidencies. Both were popular vote losers, elected as a result of the malapportioned electoral college. The initial election of both men was a turning point in the history of the respective Reconstruction – not the end itself, but the end of "forceful" federal commitment (King 2017). In a crude analogy, 2020 is 1880.

This chapter examines three key forces that are deconstructing the Second Reconstruction. The first is the rise of racially polarized partisanship, a growing and alarming trend that reintroduces the toxic partisan logic of the First Reconstruction. Once more, it is in the electoral interest of one party (this time the Republicans) to reduce non-whites' access to the ballot box, while another party (this time the Democratic Party) is increasingly reliant on non-white votes. Once more, the latter party's perceived affinity with racial minority voters serves only to expedite the departure of whites from their electoral coalition.

The second section of this chapter addresses the court's role. Since the 1970s, the Supreme Court has tried to limit voting rights and weaken civil rights statutes. Until recently, when the court acted egregiously, Congress passed new statutes to overturn the court's attacks. Congress passed a stronger version of the Voting Rights Act in 1982 to overturn the court's deconstructive ruling in *Mobile v. Bolden* (1980). It passed the Civil Rights Act of 1991 in response to *Wards*

Cove Packing Co. v. Atonio (1989) and other Supreme Court decisions that weakened the Civil Rights Act of 1964. However, since 2010, the bipartisan consensus on voting rights has evaporated, empowering the court to strike down civil rights law without fear of congressional rebuke. In 2013, the Supreme Court issued its most devastating ruling yet, rendering obsolete the most powerful enforcement tools of the Voting Rights Act of 1965. The 2016 election was the first presidential election in fifty years without the full force of the Voting Rights Act behind it.

The final section considers the consequences of this federal-level weakness at the state level. The First Reconstruction was deconstructed over a thirty-year period as states passed increasingly restrictive laws limiting African American access to the ballot box and diluting meaningful political power. Nearly all of these measures were facially race-neutral, yet they had the effect of tipping the balance of power along racial lines away from African Americans. This chapter argues that a similar process can be detected in some American states in the twenty-first century. The crippling of the Voting Rights Act by the Supreme Court has given jurisdictions the means to pursue racial disenfranchisement. Racially polarized partisanship provides the motive.

Racially Polarized Partisanship

The Second Reconstruction has survived longer than the First Reconstruction in part due to a bipartisan consensus – at least at the elite level – in favor of the keystone legislation of the Second Reconstruction: the Civil Rights Act of 1964 and the Voting Rights Act of 1965. Both laws have been renewed and strengthened by multiple administrations, including under Republican presidents. The Voting Rights Act was renewed and strengthened four times under Republican presidents: Richard Nixon, Gerald Ford, Ronald Reagan, and George W. Bush. Employment provisions in the Civil Rights Act were strengthened by Republican President George H. W. Bush in 1991. Throughout this period, there were large bipartisan majorities in Congress for these laws. As recently as 2006, overwhelming bipartisan majorities in the House (390–33) and Senate (98–0) voted to renew the Voting Rights Act and even make some of its most potent features permanent.

Such was the seeming permanence of this bipartisan consensus that in 2004 Richard Valelly felt confident enough to write that "the second [Reconstruction] proceeded so differently" from the first because "the biracial coalition is entrenched in ways that the biracial coalition in the first reconstruction never was" (2004: 16, 17). He argued that while there was a clearly white supremacist party during the First Reconstruction (the Democrats), neither party in the Second Reconstruction could be described in such a way. Pointing to George Wallace's American Independent Party, Valelly noted: "White supremacist third parties were attempted, but they were fragile and short lived"; instead, there was "really no opposing party, on site as it were, ready to impede the internal reconstruction" (2004: 18).

Valelly's assessment no longer holds. The Republican Party has increasingly defined itself not only as a party supported overwhelmingly by whites but also as one characterized by opposition to any race-conscious policy remedies to racial inequality (King and Smith 2014). Meanwhile, there has been continual "white flight" from the Democratic Party (see Figure 4.1). Barack Obama was re-elected in 2012 with the lowest share of the white two-party vote of any successfully elected president. Hillary Clinton performed even worse.

Valelly described the modern Democratic Party as "a stable biracial coalition" (2004: 231), but increasingly it resembles the Republican Party of the First Reconstruction. In many areas, the Democratic Party is overwhelmingly made up of African Americans, whereas Republican Party primaries are almost entirely all-white affairs. Nationally, both parties have become less representative of the overall racial makeup of the country. In the 1990s, the Republican party was about nine percentage points whiter than the country as a whole, while the Democratic party was about four percentage points less white. By 2012, the Republican

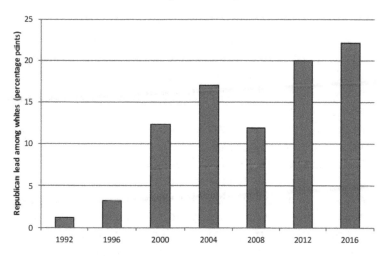

Figure 4.1: Republican lead over Democrats among whites, 1992–2016

Party was about nineteen percentage points whiter than the overall electorate, while the Democratic Party was about fifteen percentage points less white than the electorate overall (see Figure 4.2).

Because the United States is becoming less white and the

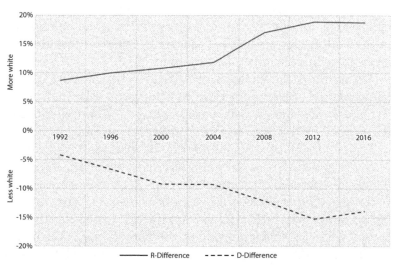

Figure 4.2: Difference between percentage of whites in the overall electorate and percentage of whites who voted for a given party, 1992–2016

Democratic electorate is also becoming less white, some commentators argue that the Democratic Party looks more like the United States. This is not quite true. It is accurate that both the Democratic electorate and the overall electorate are becoming less white at each election; they are following the same direction of change. But the Democratic Party's shrinking support among whites is happening at a faster rate than the decreasing share of whites in the overall electorate. The Democratic Party is now *less congruent* with the racial makeup of the overall electorate than it was in the 1990s (see Figure 4.3). This means that the Democrats must win even more non-white voters to make up for the lost white voters. This is not a straightforward task. The party is already close to a ceiling with African American voters (about 90 percent support).

It is not clear that the Democrats can make up the difference by courting Hispanic voters. This is due to the low turnout of Hispanic voters (about 20 percentage points lower than whites and African Americans) and is complicated by the attitudes of Hispanic *citizens* compared with those of non-citizen Hispanics, who cannot vote. Donald Trump's harsh rhetoric against illegal immigrants did him no damage among Hispanic voters. Indeed, he modestly improved Republican support among Hispanic voters, doing better than Mitt Romney had done in 2012.

Furthermore, the interests of African Americans are often distinct from other minorities. As Thurgood Marshall, the first black Supreme Court justice put it: "The experience of Negroes in America has been different in kind, not just in degree, from that of other ethnic groups." Marshall, who was married to a Filipino-heritage Hawaiian, did not disregard discrimination faced by non-black minorities, but he recognized that the history of slavery and Jim Crow in the United States separates African Americans' experience from groups who trace their history to the United States through immigration (Dawson 1994). Writer and political thinker James Baldwin put it more bluntly:

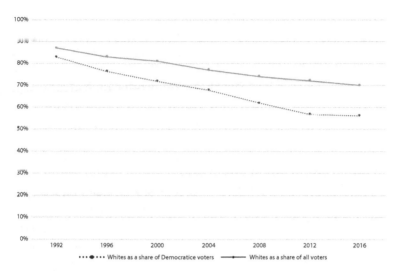

Figure 4.3: White voters as a share of the Democratic and overall electorate, 1992–2016

I had my fill of seeing people come down the gangplank on Wednesday, speaking not a word of English, and by Friday discovering that I was working for them and they were calling me nigger like everybody else. So that the Italian adventure or even the Jewish adventure, however grim, is distinguished from my adventure. (Baldwin and Mead 1971)

There has been a long-term trend in racially conservative whites moving to the Republican Party. As was discussed in Chapter 3, the departure of the Dixiecrats from the 1948 Democratic national convention was the starting gun for the racial transformation of the two main parties. It would take decades before the parties were truly reconfigured (Levendusky 2009). In the meantime, it was electorally beneficial for both parties to support the Voting Rights Act. While the successful enfranchisement of African Americans meant many new votes for the Democrats, Republicans (correctly) surmised that they could find just as many – or even more – votes from white defectors from the Democrats.

In the 1980s and 1990s, Republicans saw another reason to support the Voting Rights Act. By arguing for the creation of majority black districts, they could "bleach" other districts of the state. These "bleached" seats were more difficult for Democrats to win because they could only realistically win districts in which African Americans were at least a nontrivial minority (Bonfili 1998). The consequence was that while the number of African American legislators remained constant, the number of white Democratic legislators declined. David Lublin (1997) called this the "paradox of representation."

The consequence of these changes is that the Democratic Party, especially in the South, has increasingly been represented by non-white lawmakers. Between 1992 and 2016, the Democratic congressional caucus in the Deep South changed from being 65.2 percent white to 100 percent African American. This change is explained not by an increase in the number of black lawmakers, but by the displacement of white Democrats by white Republicans. Presenting the Democratic Party as the party "for blacks" has been a longstanding goal of Republican strategists. In 1966, Kevin Phillips, author of *The Emerging Republican Majority* (1969), the bible of the Nixon administration's political strategy, predicted that southern "white Democrats will desert their party in droves the minute it becomes a black party" (quoted in Kabaservice 2012: 274). A similar tactic was used during the First Reconstruction. Some white Democrats supported appointing the black Republican Hiram Revels to the US Senate because they thought it would tarnish the image of the Republican Party among whites.

There is little doubt that the Obama presidency accelerated these trends. When Obama became president, Democrats were only nine percentage points more likely to agree with the following statement than Republicans: "Racial discrimination is the main reason black people can't get ahead." By 2017, the gap had grown to fifty percentage points (14 percent of Republicans agreeing, compared to 64 percent of Democrats).[6] As recently as 2010, Democrats controlled half of southern state legislative chambers. By 2014, they

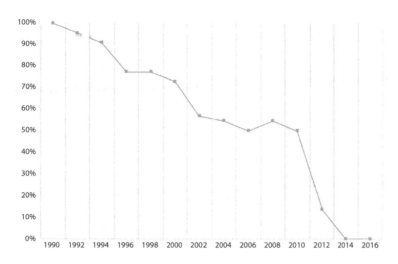

Figure 4.4: Proportion of southern state legislatures controlled by Democrats, 1990–2016
Source: National Conference of State Legislatures, South defined as the former Confederacy

controlled none of them. Within twenty-four years, the Democrats went from complete control of every legislative chamber in the former Confederacy to complete minority status (see Figure 4.4).

Judicial Deconstruction

For the most part, in the 1950s–60s, the Supreme Court was an ally of democratization. This fact has had a huge impact on contemporary scholarship about civil rights and the courts. Many scholars were educated in the glow of the Warren Court. Valelly credited the Supreme Court with "solidifying bipartisan consensus" toward the Voting Rights Act. He explained: "The Court's approval of the act strongly energized the bipartisan consensus ... It invited a virtuous circle of cooperative jurisprudence-building via the new bipartisan consensus forged by Nixon, Ford, and Reagan" (2004: 239). Yet the Warren Court was a temporary aberration from the Supreme Court's alliance with anti-democratic forces. From the 1970s onwards, the Supreme Court has largely acted to limit the reach of civil rights legislation, reduce the potency of the Reconstruction amendments, and enable hostile actors in states to reverse the democratic gains of the Second Reconstruction.

In two key rulings – *South Carolina v. Katzenbach* (1966) and *Allen v. State Board of Elections* (1969) – the Supreme Court validated the constitutionality of the Voting Rights Act. The court accurately surmised that some jurisdictions had engaged in "unremitting and ingenious defiance of the Constitution." Chief Justice Earl Warren gave Congress the green light to adopt "sterner and more elaborate measures to satisfy the clear commands of the Fifteenth Amendment." Indeed, Warren congratulated Congress for the "inventive manner" in which they had designed the Voting Rights Act. He almost provided a blank check, declaring: "Congress may use any rational means to effectuate the constitutional prohibition of racial discrimination in voting." In one of the final cases he decided before his retirement, Warren gave broad interpretation for the federal government to attack discriminatory "systems of representation." He observed: "The right to vote can be affected by a dilution of voting power as well as by an absolute prohibition on casting a ballot." This decision opened the Voting Rights Act to be used to tackle not only discriminatory devices like literacy tests but also gerrymandered electoral systems and election laws designed to dilute the voting strength of racial minorities.

Warren's departure as Chief Justice in 1969 foretold a shift in the court's civil rights jurisprudence, much as Salmon Chase's death in 1873 had done. Since the 1970s, the Supreme Court has regularly sought to reduce the potency of the Voting Rights Act and other civil rights laws (see Table 4.1). Initially, the court did this by requiring "intent-based" standards to evaluate racial discrimination. Laws and electoral systems could only be found discriminatory if plaintiffs could positively prove that the authors of such laws had explicitly designed them to discriminate against racial minorities. The authors of these discriminatory laws were dead, forcing civil rights lawyers to trawl through dusty records of municipal meetings and transcripts of bygone legislative sessions in the hope of finding the stray racist remark. Morgan Kousser (1984: 37) lamented that the Supreme Court had reduced civil rights enforcement to "the nearly impossible [search] to find guns still merrily smoking after such a long time."

One of the most savage early assaults against the Voting Rights Act came in *Mobile v. Bolden* in 1980. The court ruled that electoral systems could only be found to be in violation of the Voting Rights Act and the Fifteenth Amendment if a plaintiff could demonstrate the system was designed with the explicit purpose of racially discriminating. The *Birmingham Post-Herald* pithily mocked this standard: "Many discriminatory voting and registration rules were adopted years ago by persons who are now dead. It would be a neat trick to subpoena them from their graves for testimony about their racial motivations." Armand Derfner wrote: "*Mobile v. Bolden* brought judicial remedies for voting discrimination back to about what they had been before 1965 – largely useless" (1984: 148). The court's logic demonstrated either irresponsible insouciance or outright dishonesty. The author of the plurality opinion, Justice Potter Stewart, believed that the black plaintiffs had been "rash" to conclude that Mobile, Alabama's municipal election system, discriminated against racial minorities. Even though no African American had ever been elected to the city commission under the at-large electoral system, Stewart claimed there was no evidence that the system was designed to be racially discriminatory when it was adopted in 1911. He countered that, in fact, the at-large system (rather than ward-based elections) was commendable, writing: "It is noteworthy that a system of at-large city elections in place of elections of city officials by the voters of small geographic wards was universally heralded not many years ago as a praiseworthy and progressive reform of corrupt municipal government."

Yet Stewart flagrantly misrepresented the one source he cited to support his claim: Edward Banfield and James

Table 4.1: Judicial deconstruction of civil and voting rights during the Second Reconstruction

Case	Year	Majority	President	Chief Justice	Content
Beer v. US	1976	5–3	Gerald Ford (R)	Warren Burger	New electoral laws that preserve existing discrimination are allowed, as long as they don't create further discrimination (the "non-retrogressive standard")
Washington v. Davis	1976	7–2	Gerald Ford (R)	Warren Burger	Laws that have a racially discriminatory effect can only be found unconstitutional if it can be proven that they were written with a discriminatory purpose
Mobile v. Bolden	1980	6–3	Jimmy Carter (D)	Warren Burger	Litigants must show that an election law was designed with discriminatory intent; it is not enough to show that it has a racially discriminatory effect
Wards Cove Packing Co. v. Atonio	1989	5–4	George H W Bush (R)	William Rehnquist	Racial discrimination in employment practices is permissible if the employer can provide a business justification
Brenda Patterson v. McLean Credit Union	1989	6–3	George H W Bush (R)	William Rehnquist	Racial harassment in the workplace is not sufficient evidence to challenge non-promotion if a business case is presented
Shaw v. Reno	1993	5–4	Bill Clinton (D)	William Rehnquist	Race-conscious redistricting is unconstitutional
Miller v. Johnson	1995	5–4	Bill Clinton (D)	William Rehnquist	Race-conscious redistricting is unconstitutional
Reno v. Bossier Parish	2000	5–4	Bill Clinton (D)	William Rehnquist	Section 5 preclearance can only be used in situations which worsen racial voting dilution
Georgia v. Ashcroft	2003	5–4	George W Bush (R)	William Rehnquist	Areas under preclearance can diminish the number of majority-minority seats
NAMUDNO v. Holder	2009	8–1	Barack Obama (D)	John Roberts	The Voting Rights Act has been successful but some of its provisions might no longer be needed
Shelby County v. Holder	2013	5–4	Barack Obama (D)	John Roberts	The formula to define federal preclearance in the Voting Rights Act is unconstitutional
Rucho v. Common Cause	2019	5–4	Donald Trump (R)	John Roberts	Partisan gerrymandering is non-justiciable

Q. Wilson's classic *City Politics* (1963: 151). Banfield and Wilson do write: "[N]on-partisanship, the council-manager plan, and at-large elections are all expressions of the reform ideal and of the middle-class political ethos" (1963: 151), but what Stewart failed to acknowledge was that the authors were, in fact, *critical* of the middle-class Progressive reformers because they designed systems to disempower the working class and racial minorities. Indeed, many scholars by the mid-twentieth century chastised the classist and racist Progressive reformers. C. Vann Woodward famously titled a chapter "Progressivism – For Whites Only" in his *Origins of the New South* (1951). Stewart either deliberately mischaracterized the Banfield and Wilson book, or this rather basic insight was lost on the Supreme Court justice – itself rather worrying.

Fortunately, there was sufficient political strength in Congress to overturn the *Bolden* decision. Because the decision had been made on the basis of the court's interpretation of Section 2 of the Voting Rights Act, an amendment to that statute – rather than to the Constitution itself – would be enough to reverse the court's decision. In 1982, Congress amended the Voting Rights Act to clarify that discriminatory effect *was* sufficient grounds for a Section 2 lawsuit. Victims of discrimination would not need to spend hours parsing debates and articles written by long-dead state legislators, city councilors, and bureaucrats in order to find evidence of discriminatory "intent."

The next three decades became an ongoing battle between the anti-democratic rulings of the Supreme Court against congresses and presidents (with differing levels of commitment) who sought to restore and protect racial minorities' equal citizenship rights. By the twenty-first century, however, congressional will to rebuke the Supreme Court diminished. Due to the rise in racially polarized partisanship, bipartisan majorities needed to overturn Supreme Court rulings are not achievable. The Second Reconstruction, thus, enters a dangerous phase. The Supreme Court is now able to dilute the democratic reforms of the Second Reconstruction with impunity. Ironically, the most serious judicial challenge to the Second Reconstruction occurred during the tenure of the first black president.

A few months after Barack Obama's inauguration, the first cracks emerged. In the case *NAMUDNO v. Holder* (2009), the court openly questioned the value of the Voting Rights Act. A municipal authority (a district to elect the utility board) in Texas argued that it was unfair to be subject to Section 5 preclearance because there had been no evidence ever presented that the utility board district had discriminated against racial minorities. The court, ultimately, made a technical and narrow decision, deciding that this jurisdiction constituted a "political subdivision" which could be "bailed out" of Section 5 coverage.

While the immediate impact of *NAMUDNO v. Holder* was modest, the language of the decision was extremely ominous for the near-term viability of the Voting Rights Act. The court found that "the [Voting Rights] Act now raises serious constitutional concerns. The preclearance requirement represents an intrusion into areas of state and local responsibility that is otherwise unfamiliar to our federal system." In the court's opinion, Chief Justice John Roberts wrote, "[t]hings have changed in the South. Voter turnout and registration rates now approach parity. Blatantly discriminatory evasions of federal decrees are rare. And minority candidates hold office at unprecedented levels." In a concurring opinion, Justice Clarence Thomas opined: "Punishment for long past sins is not a legitimate basis for imposing a forward-looking preventative measure that has already served its purpose." While *NAMUDNO* kept the Voting Rights Act intact, the justices were carefully preparing for a full judicial assault in a subsequent case.

The full-on judicial attack came four years later, a few months after Barack Obama's re-election. In *Shelby County v. Holder* (2013), the court struck down Section 4 of the Voting Rights Act as unconstitutional, rendering the powerful sections that rely on it, most notably Section 5 preclearance, inoperable. Echoing Clarence Thomas's remarks in the *NAMUDNO* case, John Roberts asserted: "The [Fifteenth] Amendment is not designed to punish for the past." He argued that the racism that had justified Section 5 as a temporary and emergency measure in the 1960s had subsided. He claimed: "There is no denying, however, that the conditions that originally justified these measures no longer characterize voting in the covered jurisdictions." The court technically "issue[d] no holding on §5 itself, only on the coverage formula," but there is little question that if Section 5 was revived under a new Section 4 formula passed by Congress, it would likely be struck down anyway. Clarence Thomas wrote in his concurrence that the unconstitutionality of Section 5 is "the inevitable conclusion" of *Shelby County*.

The context of the Obama presidency is relevant to these decisions. The Obama presidency was not *coincidental to* but *a partial explanation of* the court's decision to undermine the Voting Rights Act's most powerful enforcement mechanism. The Obama elections were the culmination of the "steady march" of racial progress narrative that has been enticing to many white Americans (Klinkner and Smith 1999). The Obama elections emboldened hostile jurists to argue that the country had changed beyond recognition from the 1960s, rendering special voter protection unnecessary.

Justice Ruth Bader Ginsburg replied that a record of improvement is not in itself evidence that democratic backsliding will not occur. In a memorable phrase, Ginsburg wrote: "Volumes of evidence supported Congress' determination that the prospect of retrogression was real. Throwing out preclearance when it has worked and is continuing to work to stop discriminatory changes is like throwing away your umbrella in a rainstorm because you are not getting wet." While Ginsburg's intervention in *Shelby County* is laudable, it should be noted that she had been a supporter of the disturbing *NAMUDNO* decision, which contributed directly to *Shelby County*.

At stake in *Shelby County* was whether the Section 4 formula which Congress renewed in 2006 was a rational basis for selecting jurisdictions to place them under heightened federal monitoring for Fifteenth Amendment violations. In 2006, Congress simply preserved the formula adopted in the 1982 Voting Rights Act renewal under Ronald Reagan. The formula was largely based on data from elections in the 1960s and 1970s, but there are good reasons why these data remained relevant in the twenty-first century. The effects of an institution on subsequent institutions and behaviors can long outlast the original institution itself (Sewell 1996). Archarya and colleagues (2018) found that counties in the South where slavery was more prevalent demonstrate higher levels of racially polarized partisanship. Slave density maps from 1860 are a remarkably good predictor of southern vote strength for Obama in the 2012 election (see Figure 4.5).

Jurisdictions covered under Section 4 were areas that before the Voting Rights Act had deployed discriminatory devices to diminish non-white political participation, such as literacy tests and poll taxes. Chief Justice Roberts's claim that the Section 4 jurisdictions were no longer different from non-Section 4 jurisdictions was unsubstantiated. If this claim were true, successful lawsuits filed under Section 2, which applies to all jurisdictions, would be evenly distributed or, if anything, more concentrated in those areas that do not have the benefit of preclearance protection. Kousser (2015) has

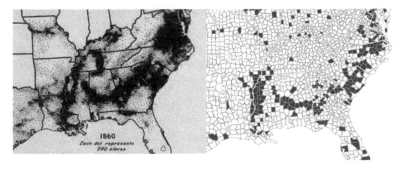

Figure 4.5: Slave density map (1860), counties won by Barack Obama in the South (2012)
Sources: US Department of Agriculture (1933: 655), author's creation

found that, on the contrary, 91.7 percent of proven voting rights violations under Section 2 litigation took place in areas that fell within the Section 4 coverage formula. Even after controlling for racial demographics (Kousser excludes areas that are more than 80 percent white), a massive difference remained between the proportion of counties which experienced successful voting rights violation law suits: 80.3 percent of counties in the Section 4 formula compared to only 11.9 percent of counties not covered by preclearance.

With respect to President Obama's election, Nathaniel Persily and colleagues (2009) found that, in the jurisdictions covered by Section 5, Obama made no gains with white voters. Persily et al. report that in the 2008 election Obama's modest increase in support in the national white vote (compared with whites' support for John Kerry in 2004) came entirely from areas not in the Section 4 formula. In the Section 4 states, the black–white racially polarized vote gap was at a high of seventy-one percentage points: 97 percent of blacks voted for Obama, while only 26 percent of whites did. In non-covered states, the gap was forty-seven percentage points. The six states with the lowest proportion of whites voting for Barack Obama were fully covered by the Section 4 formula: Alabama (10 percent white support for Obama), Mississippi (11 percent), Louisiana (14 percent), Georgia (23 percent), South Carolina (26 percent), and Texas (26 percent).

Section 2, with its intent-based standard, applies to the entire United States. It remains the last powerful mechanism of the Voting Rights Act, but it is weaker than Section 5 preclearance because it requires litigation for enforcement, which is slow and costly. In testimony to Congress arguing for Section 5 preclearance, Attorney General Nicholas Katzenbach explained in March 1965 that "what is necessary – what is essential – is a new approach, an approach which goes beyond the torturous, often ineffective pace of litigation."

Even the powers of litigation are under threat. Several of the current justices on the Supreme Court have indicated a willingness to overturn Section 2 intent-based standards.

In *Abbot v. Perez* (2018), both Clarence Thomas and Neil Gorsuch, a Trump appointee, issued an opinion stating that they did not think plaintiffs could use Section 2 to sue against racial gerrymanders. If the Roberts Court moves against the Section 2 intent-based standard, then it will have effectively dismantled the most important civil rights law in United States history.

During the Trump presidency, the Roberts Court continued the process of judicial deconstruction. In June 2019, in two combined cases (*Lamone v. Benisek* and *Rucho v. Common Cause*), the Supreme Court ruled that partisan gerrymandering was an inherently political question and therefore beyond the scope of the courts. Roberts's decision opens the floodgates to partisan gerrymandering, which will effectively disenfranchise African Americans. Roberts acknowledged that partisan gerrymandering could "lead to results that reasonably seem unjust," but Roberts refused to strike down the injustice before his eyes, disavowing that "the solution lies with the federal judiciary." He encouraged the victims of discrimination to resolve the matter through the political process, ignoring the fact that the political process itself has been skewed. Justice Elena Kagan, an Obama appointee, recognized and condemned this absurdity in her dissenting opinion. In an unusual move, Kagan read her dissent aloud:

> The majority disputes none of what I have said (or will say) about how gerrymanders undermine democracy. Indeed, the majority concedes (really, how could it not?) that gerrymandering is inconsistent with democratic principles … Of all the times to abandon the Court's duty to declare the law, this was not the one. The practices challenged in these cases imperil our system of government. Part of the Court's role in that system is to defend its foundations. None is more important than fair and free elections.

Under the *Rucho* decision, states can now legally dilute the voting strength of African Americans as long as the political actors who disenfranchise them say explicitly that they are drawing districts to dilute the *Democratic* vote rather than the black vote. In many parts of the United States, they are one and the same. The idea that partisan and racial gerrymandering can be distinguished lacks historical credence. The racist grandfather clause in the Oklahoma state constitution – which guaranteed the vote to those who descended from a person who was eligible to vote before the passage of the Civil Rights Act of 1866 – was defended on the basis that it was written "for the explicit purpose of disenfranchising negro voters not because they are black but because they vote the Republican ticket" (Bickel and Schmidt 1984: 928). It hardly matters whether the intention is racial or partisan animus. From the perspective of black voters, the effect is the same.

The re-emergence of the Supreme Court as a hostile institutional actor *without challenge* has been one of the most consequential developments of the late Second Reconstruction. In 2004, Valelly thought "the impact of that change has been fairly slight" (p. 248). On the contrary, it threatens to bring down the whole legal edifice on which the Second Reconstruction has relied.

De-Democratization in the States

Like during the First Reconstruction, much of the actual reversal of democratic institutions occurs in the individual states, partly because the United States has never truly nationalized election law or administration. Judicial attack, presidential hostility, and racially polarized partisanship are only the preconditions for state governments to restrict the franchise on racial lines for partisan gain. De-democratization in the states is occurring in three ways. First, states are increasing the barriers to registering and casting a ballot. Second, they are diluting the voting strength of racial minorities through partisan legislative districting plans. Third, opponents of the Second Reconstruction are rewriting state constitutions to change the rules of the political game to their benefit. These efforts have been actively supported by a hostile federal judiciary and, since 2016, they have been aided and abetted by the federal executive branch as well.

The *Shelby County v. Holder* decision had dramatic implications for voting rights in the South. In Section 5's forty-eight years of operation, more than three thousand attempted changes to election law and practice were blocked by the Justice Department and the DC Circuit Court (Berman 2015). The Roberts Court acknowledged that Section 5 had been incredibly effective, but, somewhat counterintuitively, Roberts concluded that it was therefore no longer necessary. Given that racially polarized partisanship was at its most intensive in the areas covered by Section 5, this logic was puzzling.

Soon after the *Shelby County* decision, jurisdictions that had heretofore been covered by Section 5 preclearance acted quickly to install new voting requirements which the Justice Department had previously blocked. In the half decade since *Shelby County*, at least 1,688 polling stations have been closed in areas previously covered by the preclearance formula. Voters have been purged from the electoral register at rates 40 percent higher than in non-Section 4 areas. States have installed myriad new requirements for registering to vote or casting a vote, the most highly publicized of which have been new voter ID laws.

During the first term of the Obama presidency, the Justice Department used Section 5 to block attempts by states to introduce overly onerous voter ID laws. Civil rights groups, such as the NAACP, argued that hundreds of thousands of voters, especially those who are poor, were rendered unable to vote because they lacked the required ID card. In Alabama alone, the NAACP estimated that more than 100,000 citizens lacked the necessary ID, the majority of whom were African American.

A particularly egregious example was a voter ID law in Texas known as SB 15. The law attracted public attention by allowing Texas gunowner permits as valid voter ID, but not ID cards issued by Texas public universities and community colleges. The law was originally blocked in 2012 under Section 5 of the Voting Rights Act; however, after the *Shelby County* decision, the state of Texas quickly acted to reintroduce the restrictions.

Left without the advantages of Section 5 preclearance, the Obama administration's Department of Justice was forced to join with civil rights groups and use Section 2 of the Voting Rights Act to sue the state of Texas in *Veasey v. Abbott* (2016). More than 600,000 Texans would be barred from voting because they lacked the requisite ID cards. African Americans were three times as likely as whites not to have the correct ID card, and Hispanics were twice as likely. For example, while 96.2 percent of white adult citizens in Texas have a driver's license, only 86.9 percent of African Americans do.

Under President Trump, the Justice Department announced that it would no longer side with the black and Hispanic litigants in the case. In spite of the executive branch's new posture, a federal judge ruled in April 2017 that the voter ID law was discriminatory. Within four months, the Texas state legislature had passed a new version of the bill, now labelled SB 5. In July 2017, a statement from the Trump Justice Department welcomed Texas's new voter ID law, claiming that "as amended by SB 5, Texas's voter ID law both guarantees to Texas voters the opportunity to cast an in-person ballot and protects the integrity of Texas's elections." The Trump Justice Department added: "SB 5 fully remedies any discriminatory effect in Texas's voter ID law."

A month later, the federal courts disagreed with the Department of Justice. Judge Nelva Gonzales Ramos of the Southern District of Texas invalidated the law on the grounds that SB 5 fell "far short of mitigating the discriminatory provisions of SB 14." Judge Ramos added: "SB 5 perpetuates the selection of types of ID most likely to be possessed by Anglo voters and, disproportionately, not possessed by Hispanics and African-Americans." Yet, upon appeal, the Fifth Circuit Court of Appeals, to which Trump has made five appointments, reversed Judge Ramos's decision. The voter ID law went into effect.

This single case shows the challenges which the disabling of Section 5 of the Voting Rights means for voting rights. Before the *Shelby County* decision, the Justice Department under the Obama administration could – and did – block the ID law under the preclearance rule. Without preclearance, the administration (and the potential victims of racial discrimination) were left to prove racial discrimination through the lengthy court process. As soon as they won one case, the Texas state legislature passed a new law and another lengthy case had to be launched.

Democracy is not only at risk in states that were covered under the Section 4 formula of the Voting Rights Act. *Shelby County v. Holder* is only part of the story. It is important for commentators not to fall into the trap of seeing state-sanctioned racism as purely a southern disease (King and Tuck 2007; Sokol 2014). In the First Reconstruction, most of the focus for democratic reformers was understandably focused on the southern states because that is where 90 percent of African Americans lived. But due to the refugee crisis known as the "Great Migration" during the twentieth century, half the black population in the United States today lives outside the South. This means that the partisan incentives for diminishing black voter participation can be as strong in the North as they once were in the South. No state has more seriously demonstrated this fact than Wisconsin.

During his governorship (2011–19), Republican Scott Walker passed thirty-three changes to Wisconsin election laws. Many of these initiatives would have been blocked by the Department of Justice under Section 5 preclearance, but because Wisconsin was not included in the Section 4 formula of the Voting Rights Act, these measures were allowed to be enacted without seeking federal approval.

Walker's changes undeniably made voting less convenient. They reduced the period in which a person could vote early from thirty days before an election to twelve days. They cut weekend and post-5 p.m. voting hours. They restricted the number of early voting polling stations to just one per municipality, meaning that small suburban towns would have the same number of polling stations as large cities such as Madison and Milwaukee. In 2012, early voters in Wisconsin delivered a seventeen percentage point margin of victory to Barack Obama in 2012; so, there was a clear partisan incentive to minimize the practice.

The Republican state legislature also sought to introduce new ID requirements, ostensibly to stop voter fraud. Spurious assertions of voter fraud were commonly cited by white supremacist state legislators during Reconstruction as the rationale for the introduction of literacy tests and other devices that disenfranchised African Americans on so-called race-neutral grounds. Revival of these claims betrayed a lack of historical knowledge, or perhaps the legislators simply did not care about the comparison.

The Wisconsin voter ID law – Wisconsin Act 23 – required voters to produce a state-issued ID card (e.g., driver's license, military license) in order to vote. ID cards for students at public universities were permissible, but only if they showed the student's signature and contained a two-year expiry date. These caveats invalidated the majority of student ID cards because it is not standard practice for them to include an electronic signature, and the two-year expiry date made little sense when the vast majority of university degrees last for four years in the United States. The new laws also stipulated new lengths for residency. In the First Reconstruction, lengthy residency requirements were used to disenfranchise African Americans who had insecure tenancies or were forced to move seasonally for work.

Civil rights groups sued the state of Wisconsin in federal court under the Voting Rights Act. In 2014, a federal district court struck down the Wisconsin voter ID law on the grounds that one in ten voters lacked the necessary ID and that most of these – especially people who couldn't drive – were likely to be poor. In a state like Wisconsin, where 37 percent of black people live in poverty, it was, therefore, unsurprising that African Americans were 50 percent less likely to possess the new ID documents. District court judge Lynn Adelman, a Clinton-appointee, found in *Frank v. Walker* (2014) that the law introduced unacceptable barriers to voting, which disproportionately affected non-white voters. He ruled: "It is absolutely clear that [the law] will prevent more legitimate votes from being cast than fraudulent votes." Judge Adelman's ruling was overturned on appeal to the Seventh Circuit Court by a panel of three judges, all whom were appointed by either Ronald Reagan or George W. Bush.

In 2016, under renewed litigation, a federal district court ruled against the law on the grounds that state bureaucrats had disproportionately denied requests for voter ID to racial minorities. It was revealed that a staggering 88 percent of those who had been denied voter ID by state officials at the Department for Motor Vehicles were black or Hispanic. District court judge James Peterson, an Obama-appointee, called the voter ID law "a wretched failure" and "manifestly inadequate." He added that the voting changes were passed "to suppress the reliably Democratic vote of Milwaukee's African Americans ... The Wisconsin experience ... demonstrates that a preoccupation with mostly phantom election fraud leads to real incidents of disenfranchisement, which undermine rather than enhance confidence in elections, particularly in minority communities."

The federal circuit court, however, declared that the Peterson ruling from the district level did not need to be implemented before the 2016 election, allowing the voter ID law to stand at this crucial stage. The consequences of this decision were profound, not only on Wisconsin politics but also, due to the electoral college, for national politics.

Wisconsin has historically been a bastion of American social democracy. Like nearby Minnesota and North Dakota, the state had a tradition of "prairie populism," electing social democratic third-party candidates to major office in the interwar period (Valelly 1989; Lebedoff 1969; Mitau 1970). Milwaukee elected socialists to Congress, the city council, and the mayoralty. Their closest international analogue was the Cooperative Commonwealth Federation, which became the present-day New Democratic Party (NDP), in Canada (Lipset 1950). Some commentators have credited the upper

Midwest's high proportion of Scandinavian immigrants in the early twentieth century for having imported a social democratic ethos to the region. In recent history, the state has voted consistently for Democratic presidential candidates. Between 1988 and 2012, it voted Democratic at every presidential election.

The state also has a strong tradition of civic and electoral participation. In 2008 and 2012, Wisconsin had the second highest voter turnout in the United States, second only to neighboring Minnesota in both instances. It slipped four places in 2016, as ninety-one thousand fewer people voted compared to the 2012 election. Forty-one thousand of these "missing" votes were in the staunchly Democratic and predominantly African American city of Milwaukee. Donald Trump won the state by twenty-three thousand votes. Counties that saw the biggest decline in the vote between 2012 and 2016 were also the ones with the largest proportions of African Americans (see Figure 4.6).

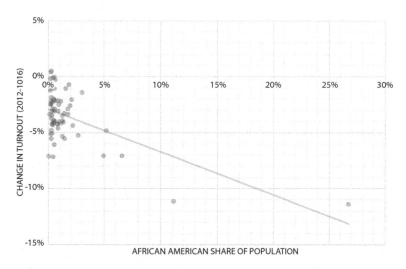

Figure 4.6: Change in turnout in Wisconsin counties (2012–16), sorted by black population
Source: Turnout data from Wisconsin Elections Commission; racial demographic data from US Census

There are myriad explanations why Hillary Clinton lost Wisconsin, not least her decision not to campaign in the state even once during the lead-up to the election (Allen and Parnes 2017), but a study based on survey data, by Kenneth Mayer and Michael DeCrescenzo (2017), estimated that forty-five thousand Wisconsin voters did not go to the polls in 2016 because of the voter ID law, a figure nearly double that of Trump's majority.

Defenders of the voter ID law argue that it worked as intended. Seventy felons were caught trying to vote, and sixteen other instances of vote fraud were blocked. Yet, one might wonder whether these eighty-six cases of wrongful voting justify a system that deterred forty-five thousand rightful voters. Racially polarized partisanship gives the Republican state government a strong incentive to introduce a device designed, as Judge James Peterson put it, "to suppress the reliably Democratic vote of Milwaukee's African Americans." On that measure, it was a manifest success.

The zealous removal of "inactive" voters from the electoral register has been another way in which states have attempted to limit the franchise for partisan-racial gain. States have removed "inactive" or "ineligible" voters, often in areas with high Democratic – and, therefore, minority – electorates. The result is that legally registered voters are removed from the electoral rolls without their knowledge or consent.

Defenders argue that such policies are necessary to maintain accurate voting records. Some defenders have also argued that higher barriers to registration prevent the lazy and indolent from voting, a normatively desirable goal. John Merrill, the Republican official in charge of Alabama's election laws, argued: "If you're too sorry or lazy to get up off of your rear and to go register to vote ... and then to go vote, then you don't deserve that privilege. As long as I'm Secretary of State of Alabama, you're going to have to show some initiative to become a registered voter in this state." A UN report published in 2018 showed that the United States is one of the most difficult countries in which to register to vote. Only 64 percent of eligible Americans are registered to vote, compared to 91 percent in the United Kingdom, 91 percent in Canada, 96 percent in Sweden, and 99 percent in Japan.[7]

Before the Trump administration, presidential administrations of both parties attempted to encourage voter registration and protect those already placed on the electoral roles. The National Voter Registration Act of 1993, passed by President Bill Clinton, and the Help American Vote Act of 2002, passed by President George W. Bush, were designed to widen voting participation. Since their passage, administrations have interpreted provisions in these laws as prohibiting states from using voter inactivity as a trigger for purging a person from the electoral register. In other words, the Clinton, Bush, and Obama administrations all agreed that failure to vote should not be a reason in itself to cancel someone's registered voter status.

The state of Ohio, however, passed legislation that does precisely this. The state removes voters from the electoral register if they fail to vote in two consecutive election cycles. If someone voted for Obama or McCain in 2008 but sat out the 2012 presidential election, by the time of the 2016 election, under the Ohio law, that voter would be deregistered unless new action was taken. In 2016, the Sixth Circuit Court blocked the measure from taking full effect before the presidential election, and the case (*Husted v. A. Philip Randolph Institute*, 2018) reached the Supreme Court shortly after President Trump placed Neil Gorsuch on the bench.

Donald Trump's solicitor general, Noel Francisco, sided with the state of Ohio against the civil rights groups that contested the vote purging tactics. During oral arguments in January 2018, Justice Sonia Sotomayor pressed the solicitor general to explain why the Trump administration had ignored the precedent set by Presidents Clinton, Bush, and Obama. Sotomayor stated:

There's a 24-year history of solicitor generals of both political parties ... who have taken a position contrary to yours ...

[It] seems quite unusual that your office would change its position so dramatically ... After that many Presidents, that many solicitor generals, this many years – the vast majority of states ... who read it the way your opponents read it, most people read it that way – how did the solicitor general change its mind?

Adding to Sotomayor's query, Justice Ruth Bader Ginsberg puzzled during oral argument: "I thought that the United States [i.e., the federal government] was taking the position, consistently, that non-voting was not a reliable indicator of residence change." Francisco confirmed that, indeed, "our prior position was based on an understanding of the statute that read into it a reliable evidence requirement, and we said that non-voting was not that kind of reliable evidence." But, Francisco then declared that the Trump administration had re-read the relevant statutes and concluded that the previous administrations were simply wrong in their interpretation.

In June 2018, in a 5–4 decision, the five Republican-appointed justices voted to confirm the constitutionality of the Ohio vote purging methods. In her dissent, Justice Sotomayor decried that the court was "sanctioning the very purging that Congress expressly sought to protect against." The ruling, she wrote, "upholds a program that appears to further the very disenfranchisement of minority and low-income voters that Congress set out to eradicate." In the court's opinion, Justice Samuel Alito retorted: "Justice Sotomayor's dissent says nothing about what is relevant in this case." He thought Sotomayor was "misconceived" in citing racial discrimination in her decision, seeing that there was no explicit racial animus from the legislators who wrote the purging law. Ominously, Alito asserted that he believed discriminatory *intent*, not effect, was required to find the practice unconstitutional. He concluded: "Justice Sotomayor has not pointed to any evidence in the record that Ohio instituted or has carried out its program with discriminatory intent."

Punitive voter ID laws and overzealous voter purges are relatively new innovations in efforts to restrict access to the ballot box. They have been used because many of the methods adopted to disenfranchise African Americans during the Jim Crow era – poll taxes, literacy tests, grandfather clauses, all-white primaries – were banned by the Voting Rights Act, the Twenty-Fourth Amendment, or earlier court rulings. Yet, while the Voting Rights Act was transformative in many ways, it did not ban all practices written during the Jim Crow era to disenfranchise African Americans.

During the Jim Crow era, "felon disenfranchisement" laws were introduced as a means of depriving the vote from, especially, African Americans through a facially race-neutral method (see Uggen and Manza 2002; Behrens et al. 2003; Manza and Uggen 2006; Lerman and Weaver 2014). These laws were not overturned by the Voting Rights Act. As Michelle Alexander (2012) writes in *The New Jim Crow*, once an American is given "felon" status, old forms of discrimination become legal: the denial of social housing, welfare benefits, jury service, the right to vote, access to jobs, and educational opportunities. More than five million Americans are "felons," disproportionately African Americans.

Former felons can experience the deprival of equal citizenship even after they have completed their sentence. Thirty-one states and the federal government impose lifetime bans on ex-felons serving on juries, which has resulted in nearly one-third of black men being ineligible from jury service in the United States (Alexander 2012: 121). In three states (Virginia, Kentucky, and Iowa), all ex-felons experience lifetime bans on voting. Six more states (Mississippi, Alabama, Tennessee, Arizona, Nevada, and Wyoming) ban most ex-felons from voting for life.

In Mississippi, one in four black men cannot vote (Chin 2002: 422). The state delivers lifetime voting bans for a range of crimes, including theft. As a result, 166,000 Mississippians who have completed their prison sentences cannot vote for the rest of their lives (Uggen et al. 2016: 15). The federal courts have embraced the constitutionality of these laws. In Mississippi, there is no question that the felon disenfranchisement provisions were written into the state constitution to disenfranchise African Americans. Indeed, state officials in 1896 were open about the fact that the provisions were designed "to obstruct the exercise of the franchise by the Negro race" (*Ratliff v. Beale*, 1896). While in this case discriminatory *intent* was obvious, a federal court in 1998 ruled that discriminatory *effect* was no longer clear. Therefore, because the law applied to all felons equally, the federal court was satisfied that the law was no longer used in a racially discriminatory way, in spite of its indisputably racist origins (*Cotton v. Fordice*, 1998).

The Mississippi electoral system is particularly unreconstructed. Its constitution was written at the end of the First Reconstruction in order to disenfranchise African Americans. The deconstructive intent of the framers of Mississippi's 1890 constitution was no secret. One of its authors, James Vardaman, was candid: "There is no use to equivocate or lie about the matter. Mississippi's constitutional convention was held for no other purpose than to eliminate the nigger from politics."[8] Even the white supremacist governor Theodore Bilbo described it as a constitution "that damn few white men and no niggers at all can explain" (Newton 2010: 53).

The process for electing the governor is one designed by these convoluted rules in the 1890 constitution geared toward minimizing black power. Statewide elections in Mississippi have an insurance clause for candidates supported by whites. In order to be elected governor, a candidate must both command majority support in the electorate *and* win a majority of state legislative districts. If a candidate cannot satisfy both requirements, then the state legislature chooses the new governor. The rule was created out of concern that the mass electorate in Mississippi might elect a pro-civil rights governor, showing once more that Jim Crow was not a case of "majority tyranny," but instead dependent on shrunken electorates formed by anti-democratic structures, which prioritize territorial representation over core democratic principles of "one vote, one value."

In 1999, Democrat Ronnie Musgrove won the most votes in the Mississippi gubernatorial election, but a majority of the vote in only 61 out of 122 state legislative districts, one district short of the segregationist constitution's require-ments. The election was thrown to the Mississippi House of Representatives, where the Democrats controlled the majority. They dutifully voted for Musgrove to be governor.

In 2019, Democrats were optimistic that they could win back the governor's mansion for the first time since Musgrove. Their candidate, Jim Hood, had been an effective state attorney general, with strong support from the state's African American population. In 2005, Hood prosecuted Ku Klux Klan member Edgar Ray Killen for the 1964 murders of three civil rights activists who were killed trying to register black Mississippians to vote. Hood's prosecution resulted in Killen being found guilty of the manslaughter of James Chaney, Michael Schwerner, and Andrew Goodman nearly forty-years after their grisly deaths. Killen died in prison at the age of ninety-two in 2018.

Some polls showed Hood in the lead against his Republican rival Tate Reeves, but the Democrats' optimism was misplaced. In reality, due to the historic rules of the anti-Reconstruction Mississippi constitution and recent partisan gerrymandering, Hood's candidacy was always doomed. After winning full control of the Mississippi state legislature in 2011 for the first time since the First Reconstruction, Republicans redrew legislative district boundaries to favor their own party. In the subsequent state legislative elections, Republicans won 63 percent of seats. The gerrymandered districts were so uncompetitive that, in 2019, only 22 out of 122 legislative districts had contested elections between the two parties. In the remaining 100 seats, candidates either stood unopposed or faced tokenistic opposition from minor parties. Even if Jim Hood had won a majority of the popular vote, he was still destined to lose because he was very unlikely to win a majority in 62 state legislative districts. For the foreseeable future, even a Republican who loses the popular vote in Mississippi can expect to become governor anyway.

An electoral structure that blocks Democrats from winning high office has direct policy consequences for

African Americans. In yet another judicial attack on the working class and racial minorities, in *NFIB v. Sebelius* (2012), the Supreme Court ruled that states could refuse to expand access to Medicaid to all households earning less than 138 percent of the federal poverty level, in spite of the Obamacare legislation that provided these states with the funding to do so. As of 2019, 75 percent of the former Confederate states have used the *Sebelius* decision to block the expansion of Medicaid to their working-class, disproportionately African American, residents. In comparison, only 17 percent of non-Confederate states have refused to expand Medicaid.

Mississippi is one of fourteen states whose governors have used the Supreme Court's *NFIB v. Sebelius* ruling to prevent the expansion of Medicaid to the working class, depriving 103,000 Mississippians of publicly provided healthcare (Garfield et al. 2019). These citizens are disproportionately African American. While Jim Hood vowed to implement Medicaid expansion, his Republican opponent made it clear he would not. At one campaign event, Steve Reeves chanted repeatedly, "I am opposed to Obamacare expansion in Mississippi. I am opposed to Obamacare expansion in Mississippi. I am opposed to Obamacare expansion in Mississippi."[9] Reeves ended up winning the election in November 2019, securing 53 percent of the vote to Hood's 47 percent. But, even if the voting totals had been reversed – if Hood had won 53 percent of the vote – it is very unlikely that Hood would have become governor. The Republican state legislature would have overturned the popular vote in favor of a losing Republican candidate.

These examples show that while the Voting Rights Act of 1965 was transformative to African American electoral participation, it was not sufficient. In his *Shelby County* decision, John Roberts lauded the fact that the Act had been "immensely successful at redressing racial discrimination ... Our country has changed." In reality, pockets of Jim Crow voting discrimination were allowed to continue, even under the Voting Rights Act. Some formal barriers from the collapse of the First Reconstruction were never eradicated during the Second Reconstruction.

Conclusion

In the United States, access to the franchise has always been shaped in partisan terms. The politics of suffrage has never been a simple matter of a progressive expansion of the right to vote. Access to the ballot has been increased and shrunk according to whoever manages to win power to write the rules. In the twenty-first century, when party and race so closely align, rules written to advantage one party inevitably seek to advantage a race. Rules with seemingly innocuous, race-neutral purposes, such as requiring voters to provide a state-issued photo ID to vote, can have racial and partisan implications if groups have access to those IDs at different rates.

While the Voting Rights Act of 1965 outlawed many racist electoral rules, some of them have been preserved. Worse, the mechanisms to enforce the prohibition of the devices that *were* banned by the act have been severely weakened by judicial deconstruction. The Voting Rights Act was instrumental to modern American democratic state-building. It is impossible to imagine the election of the first black president or the successful re-enfranchisement of millions of African Americans without it. But its fate also underscores that democratization in the United States is not a linear process. It has been marked by failures and reversals as much as by successful progressions. The "stabilization" that Richard Valelly (2004: 223) argued characterized the Second Reconstruction now appears to be a chimera.

5

Reconstructing Reconstruction

Since we have discerned that the victory of the Free States ...
will strike off the fetters of the slave, you have attracted our
warm and earnest sympathy. We joyfully honour you as the
President, and the Congress with you, for many decisive steps
towards practically exemplifying your belief in the words of
your great founders, "all men are created free and equal."
... thus for ever renouncing that unworthy prejudice which
refuses the rights of humanity to men and women on account
of their colour.

Letter of the Working-Men of Manchester,
England, to Abraham Lincoln (1864)

Carol Moseley Braun's career spanned both white and black
worlds. Her grandparents had been supporters of the black
nationalist Marcus Garvey, "race men, as they were called at
the time."[1] In an article for the black magazine *Ebony*, she
recalled that her parents "raised us in a world that did not
acknowledge or legitimize racism. Ethnic pride was part and
parcel of this world."[2] As a youth, Braun marched alongside
Martin Luther King on two occasions against housing
discrimination in her native Chicago.[3] She also engaged in
protests as a student, refusing to leave an all-white café

until she was served, and going swimming at a segregated beach (Gutgold 2006).[4] Although she never joined the Black Panthers, she was a volunteer at the Black Panthers' free breakfast program, which distributed meals to hundreds of Chicago's children every day (Witt 2007: 35).[5] She was also active in anti-apartheid work.[6]

Proud of her racial identity, Braun was not a black separatist, as some of her fellow South Siders were. She had a degree from the prestigious University of Chicago Law School and settled in Hyde Park, a predominantly white enclave in the black South Side. After working in the US attorney's office, she was encouraged to run for the Illinois House of Representatives by local left-wing whites. Braun came from a politically active family – her father had been an ally of the local alderman Leon Despres, who was a socialist and labor organizer. Although Despres was white, Braun jokingly called him "the best black alderman ever because he was one of the few who would stand up to Daley on behalf of issues touching the black community."[7] In this vein, the *Negro Digest* called Despres "the lone 'negro' spokesman in Chicago's city council."[8]

In the fall of 1991, President George H. W. Bush nominated Clarence Thomas to the Supreme Court. Thomas was an African American and would be filling the seat held by the court's first black justice, Thurgood Marshall. Thomas, however, had spent his political career downplaying the federal government's role in remedying material racial inequalities. A believer in a conservative form of "black pessimism," Thomas rejected any redistributive efforts by the state to correct centuries of racial oppression (Robin 2019).

Illinois's two-term Democratic Senator Alan Dixon was considering his options. A self-described "moderate" and "friend of business," Dixon had already angered liberals by his support for anti-abortion legislation and financial deregulation (Kenney and Hartley 2012). Braun, who by this point was a county official, met with Dixon to plead that he vote against Thomas's nomination. Braun recalled their meeting:

The conversation from my end was why Clarence Thomas was so inappropriate as a successor to Thurgood Marshall. And, I went to great lengths to explain the civil rights issue; what was involved with those of us who had marched; how important Thurgood Marshall had been in my life ... The Warren Court made such a huge difference for a little black girl like me that I felt that it was imperative that the next African American Supreme Court justice be worthy to fill the shoes of Thurgood Marshall and that Bush's nominee Clarence Thomas in no way fit that description. Now I mean I was passionate, and see I still get passionate about it because that was just a deal killer for me. And I tried to talk to Dixon in terms of, *Don't you understand that to allow Clarence Thomas to become the successor to Thurgood Marshall is essentially to deny all the sacrifices of all these people who have been pushing in the direction of equality for black people?* And this is just wrong on that front. I had [a] second meeting with Dixon in that period. And again, the same plea, *Please, please, please, please, please don't do this. You know this is wrong for civil rights reasons.*[9]

Alan Dixon ignored Braun's pleas. On October 15, 1991, Dixon was one of eleven Democrats to vote to confirm Clarence Thomas's nomination to the Supreme Court, which passed narrowly (52–48). Dixon soon came to regret this vote. His phone didn't stop ringing, as long-time supporters told him they would not support him for re-election. One fundraiser told him: "Alan, I am not going to help you, and I don't want lunch. My God, even Howell Heflin of Alabama voted against Clarence Thomas. In fact, I want you to know that I am going to do all I can to send you back to Belleville" (Dixon 2013: 307).

Female members of the Illinois Democratic State Central Committee stated that they would not support Dixon's nomination for a third term. Within weeks, Carol Moseley Braun was recruited to challenge Dixon by the same, mostly white, Hyde Parkers, who had encouraged her to run for the Illinois House of Representatives in 1978.[10] In a shocking upset, Braun defeated Dixon in the Democratic primary, and then went on to win the general election. In so doing, Braun made history: she was the first black Democrat ever to be elected to the US Senate.

Unsurprisingly, Braun won the 1992 general election with 95 percent of the black vote. Her victory, however, extended far beyond the black community. Nearly 75 percent of her support came from white voters, and she out-polled her Republican opponent in the twenty-eight Illinois counties with virtually no (less than 1 percent) racial minorities. She also outpolled presidential candidate Bill Clinton by 177,776 votes. Overall, Braun won 48 percent of the white vote.

The Braun campaign did not write off white working-class voters as potential participants in her coalition. The campaign recognized that they could be difficult to persuade – that as a black woman, Braun would have to work extra hard to reach these white working-class men and women. But the campaign also understood not to use voters' perceived social attitudes as an excuse not to try. I have been given unique access by Senator Braun to her campaign's internal strategy documents, which are otherwise embargoed until 2048. I reproduce below a relevant section from a strategy memo from my archival research:

> The so-called Reagan Democrats:
>
> These voters have Democratic demographics and lifestyles, but have often been split away from voting Democratic in recent years by appeals to race, cultural issues, defense/ foreign affairs issues, and taxes ... However these voters are usually the most concerned with African-Americans, and may be nervous about a woman Senator. In addition, they are the Republicans' prime targets for negative advertising.
>
> So, CMB is going to have to do her own persuasion of these voters, to get them to vote for her – positive persuasion which emphasizes change, populist economics, anti-elite and anti-Washington themes, and hard core Democratic issues like jobs, health care, and education.
>
> And perhaps negative persuasion which would focus on RW [Republican opponent Richard Williamson] as a wealthy

DC insider who has consistently manipulated the system for his own selfish ends, who waffles on fundamental issues, and who has served the rich and powerful throughout his career.

Issues – populist economics; anti-Bush, anti-GOP links with [Ross] Perot; invest in America, take care of our own; change in DC.

At the same time, Braun never eschewed her racial identity or tried to "deracialize." When her Republican opponent accused her of being a welfare cheat, she hit back. At a press conference, she stated that the Republicans had "attempted to peddle racism" and were "trying to frighten people with the image of a bomb-throwing welfare mother running for the Senate" (Gutgold 2006: 144).[11] Braun, herself, contends that she had no qualms about the strategy:

> I've always been very straightforward about [race] – I've never hid that light under a bushel. I feel if I'm in a room, part of the value I bring to that room is a perspective based on the fact that I am female with brown skin. Otherwise, I may just as well be another white guy, no offence, but you see what I'm saying? What's the point? If I'm not going to articulate and give voice to the set of experiences that are defining for me, then I have no legitimacy. So, calling it a racial attack, I had no problem doing that because that's exactly what it was.[12]

Braun's strong antiracism did not lead her to overlook or deny the concerns of the white working class, either. She spent her political career building deep connections with rural, working-class voters in downstate Illinois. Downstate includes a mix of rust belt industrialism, a plains agriculture economy, and even a Mississippi River floodplain. The far south of the state, as one Braun campaign worker described it, "in general is like Mississippi, and it's physically closer to Mississippi than it is to Chicago."[13] Since the late 1970s, as a state legislator, Braun had worked to support redistributive policies for rural Illinoisans. In fact, she argues that she had closer ties with downstate legislators than with

Chicago legislators who ostracized her for her anti-machine politics.[14] As a black, non-machine politician, Braun was a political outsider. She used her outsider status to find common cause with working-class voters – both in black and brown communities in Chicago and in rural white communities. Her campaign was a triumph of multiracial populism.

* * *

Carol Moseley Braun's election to the Senate is an important, but often overlooked, milestone in American racial history. Her place in history is often overshadowed by Barack Obama. Braun's political career shares many similarities with the adopted Chicagoan. They both worked at the same civil rights law firm. They were both connected to the University of Chicago Law School. They both lived in and represented the same community (Hyde Park) in the state legislature. They held the same US Senate seat. Braun was the first black Democratic senator; Barack Obama was the second. The connections run deeper. Fresh from his presidency of the *Harvard Law Review*, Obama turned down a prestigious judicial clerkship for the Chief Judge of the DC Circuit Court to help Braun's 1992 campaign register African Americans to vote (Johnson 2017). Obama only decided to run for the Senate in 2004 after he was given reassurances that Braun would not try to win back her seat (Axelrod 2015).

Yet, in many ways, Braun is perhaps the more instructive figure for the next stage of American politics. She was deeply rooted in civil rights and labor politics. Both these links helped her to forge a coalition of working-class African Americans and working-class whites. What is evident when reading Braun's strategy document in light of the 2016 election is that Illinois native Hillary Clinton manifestly failed to put across a similar message. Clinton performed disastrously in many of the very same counties that had once been carried by a black Democratic woman from Chicago (see Figure 5.1).

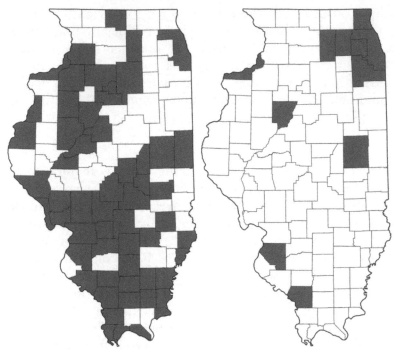

Figure 5.1: Counties won by Carol Moseley Braun in 1992 (left) and Hillary Clinton in 2016 (right)
Source: Author's creation

Clinton did not maintain the same message discipline as Braun on the "core Democratic issues," and she was unable to overcome the "DC insider" image, which Braun used so effectively against her Republican opponent. Indeed, Braun's campaign script ("invest in America," "take care of our own") could have formed parts of Donald Trump's message to working-class whites. Yet, as the Braun campaign shows, there is no reason why a Democratic candidate cannot articulate these themes while remaining committed to other key principles of equality and social justice. It is an unapologetically populist message, from an antiracist black woman, which the Democrats would do well to rediscover.

This chapter argues that multiracial populism must be the political answer to the crisis of the Second Reconstruction. The death of the Second Reconstruction is not total, nor is it the irreversible destiny of American democracy. There are steps that can be taken to reverse it. These efforts must involve a cross-racial alliance – one that does not ignore or downplay enduring racial inequalities, but at the same time invites economically depressed and politically cynical whites to find common cause against political corruption and rally together for social and economic justice. The first section of this chapter will elaborate on the politics of "reconstructing Reconstruction" through multiracial populism. The second section acknowledges, however, that multiracial populism is only part of the solution. For the long-term viability of multiracial democracy in the United States, the undemocratic institutions in the Constitution must be dislodged. At the heart of both Reconstructions was a failure to overhaul the undemocratic and, frankly, racist elements of the US constitutional order. The politics of multiracial populism is a necessary precondition to bring about these far-reaching structural reforms.

Multiracial Populism

In the Trump era, attacking populism has been a favored pastime of liberal commentators. Cas Mudde, Jan-Werner Müller, Pippa Norris, and others have written elaborate treatises decrying the authoritarianism which they believe is implicit in populism. For them, there is something inherently sinister and illiberal about populism. Müller, for example, argues: "The danger to democracy today is not some comprehensive ideology that systematically denies democratic ideals. The danger is populism – a degraded form of democracy" (2016: 9).

These definitions have their origins in discredited histories of the original 1880s and 1890s American populist movements, most influentially articulated by mid-twentieth-century liberal academics Richard Hofstadter (1955);

Daniel Bell (1964); Edward Shils (1956); and Seymour Martin Lipset (1963). Bell aligned populism with the twentieth-century far right: "the radical right of the early 1960s is in no way different from the Populists of the 1890s" (1964: 46). Lipset aligned populism with fascism and Nazism (1963: 131, 169). He erroneously drew a genealogy from the 1890s populists to Joseph McCarthy and his form of virulent, exclusionary politics (1963: 170). Shils denounced populism as "an irrational protest ideology" (1956: 98).

These scholars feared populism because they, in effect, did not trust the mass public. The liberal commentator Walter Lippmann betrayed these feelings when he wrote: "The mass public [is] not merely uninterested and uninformed, but [is] a powerful force that [is] so out of sync with reality as to constitute a massive and potentially fatal threat to effective government and policies" (1955: 20). Michael Kazin accurately surmised that the "great fear of liberal intellectuals" was the workers who "had been the foot soldiers in causes such as industrial unionism, the CIO, and the Popular Front in the 1930s and 1940s" (1995: 287).

Far from being right-wing fascists, these populist groups of working-class people were organized to attack fascism and racism. The communist Earl Browder, leader of the left-wing and patriotic American Popular Front in the 1930s and 1940s, was also a fierce antiracist and integrationist. He wrote in a 1944 article: "All the decisive forces of history are now working for Negro equality, and we Communists must strengthen our collaboration with these progressive forces of which we are a vital part." He called for "integrating the Negro people into the general democracy of our country, on the basis of complete and un-conditional equality." Showing that memory of the failure of the First Reconstruction was still fresh, Browder added: "We have today to establish the guarantees that there will not be a disappointment such as was administered by the Republican Party after the Civil War" (1944: 84, 85).

In their zeal to delegitimize populism, mid-twentieth-century liberal commentators cast aside its bold multiracialism. The first self-described populists were at their highest strength in the 1880s and 1890s. They were not antidemocrats. They were brave fighters for multiracial American democracy. They promoted a politics of the many, not the few.

During the First Reconstruction, heroic efforts by grassroots activists resulted in localized successes in overthrowing white supremacy. Black Republicans and white working-class Populists allied together to defeat bourgeois white supremacy in state and local elections throughout the South. Well into the 1890s, two decades after their abandonment by the federal government, African Americans continued to stand for election, work with sympathetic whites, publish political pamphlets and newspapers, and attempt to cast ballots in elections, often in the face of immense economic sanction or threat of physical violence. As the First Reconstruction came to a close, it is important to underscore that African Americans were not quiescent in the face of the efforts to strip away their political power.

Multiracial partisan politics was key to this resistance. The end of Reconstruction saw one brief period in which an alternative political future could have been realized. White dissatisfaction grew with the Democratic Party in many parts of the South in the post-Civil War years. The suppression of black power had not resulted in large material gains for the region's poor whites. By the 1880s, about half of the white farmers in some parts of the South were landless share-croppers – a similar material condition to the vast majority of southern African Americans (Flynt 2004: 6).

State-level populist parties in Virginia, Texas, North Carolina, and Alabama emerged in response to this economic precariousness. Unlike the Democrats, the Populists regarded a multiracial alliance as complementary to their policy goals and "came to see a common cause" (Gerteis 2003: 202). In the 1890s, many of these parties agreed to "fuse" their tickets with black Republicans to assist them in local and state elections. Keeanga-Yamahtta Taylor (2008) writes that the "Populist movement showed the possibility of a united struggle."

In 1892, the Virginia People's Party urged the black and white working classes to support them. The *Virginia Sun*, the party's newspaper, extolled that "reformers of both colors can meet on common ground, for the common good." It predicted that, under populism, "the color line will be eliminated from politics."[15] While the Virginian populists were mostly electorally unsuccessful, in neighboring North Carolina, a fusion of black Republicans and white Populists won control of the state legislature in the 1894 election, and in 1896 Republican Daniel Russell was elected governor – overturning two decades of white supremacist, Democratic rule. In 1892 and 1894, Populist Reuben Kolb would have become governor of Alabama had it not been for "rampant ballot tampering." It was the success of this multiracial alliance that led white supremacist Democrats in 1901 to change the state constitution, inserting poll taxes and literacy tests, which blocked not only African Americans but also many poor whites from voting. One convention delegate explained that he was comfortable with provisions that "might disenfranchise one or two bastards in the white counties of Alabama" (Forner 2017: 9).

Unity existed not only at the ballot box but also on the picket line. The most remarkable example of multiracial working-class solidarity was the 1892 New Orleans general strike. As Daniel Rosenberg writes: "White and Black trade unionists in New Orleans had coalesced politically in the 1880s. New Orleans workers carried out a massive, united general strike in 1892 and cooperated interracially over a ten-year span" (1988: 9).

These largely forgotten episodes are an important corrective to the dominant narrative in contemporary academic writing that portrays "populism" as an inherently anti-democratic, racist form of politics. Populist politics – defined by appeals to working-class political activism, opposition to moneyed elites, and dedication to reforming unrepresentative political institutions – can be a crucial driving force of democratization and democracy's endurance.

There are multiple reasons why the coalition of black Republicans and white Populists ultimately faltered. Centrally, it was due to the scale of white supremacist violence, which had no counter from the federal government. By the time that the multiracial Populists were challenging the white supremacist Democrats, it had been a decade since the last federal troops were pulled out of the South in the Compromise of 1877. W. E. B. Du Bois sullenly observed:

> White labor in the Populist movement of the eighties tried to realign the economic warfare in the South and bring workers of all colors into united opposition to the employer [the plantation class]. But they found that the power which they had put in the hands of the employer in 1876 so dominated political life that free and honest expression of public will at the ballot box was impossible in the South, even for white men. (1935: 353)

White supremacists' intense opposition to this multiracial populism was evident in their response to a relatively trivial municipal election in North Carolina. In 1898, a biracial coalition of black Republicans and white Populists was elected to Wilmington City Council. A mob of white Democrats burned down the headquarters of the local black newspaper and murdered as many as sixty African Americans. Thousands more fled, and the lawful election results were overturned.

Those committed to the endurance of democracy in the United States must be willing to engage in a similar strategy of multiracial populism. Commentators have been too quick to dismiss the possibility that candidates can "enlarge" the white public's understanding of racism and poverty without diminishing the legitimacy of their own material concerns. Some of the most skillful practitioners of this approach have been black Democratic politicians, as Carol

Moseley Braun shows. They stand in a proud tradition of multiracial populism, which produced the fiercest resistance to the forces of white supremacy at the end of the First Reconstruction. Some of the most popular politicians among African American voters in recent times – Barack Obama and, it appears, Bernie Sanders in 2020 – are proponents of multiracial populism.

At a North American leaders' conference in June 2016, Obama embraced the populist label and drew a conceptual distinction between populism and racism:

> I think there should be curbs on the excesses of our financial sector so that we don't repeat the debacles of 2007 and 2008. I think there should be transparency in how our systems work so that we don't have people dodging taxes … I suppose that makes me a populist. Now, somebody else who has never shown any regard for workers, has never fought on behalf of social justice issues or making sure that poor kids are getting a decent shot at life or have health care – in fact, have worked against economic opportunity for workers and ordinary people – they don't suddenly become a populist because they say something controversial in order to win votes. That's not the measure of populism. That's nativism. Or xenophobia. Or worse. Or it's just cynicism. So I would just advise everybody to be careful about suddenly attributing to whoever pops up at a time of economic anxiety the label that they're populist. Where have they been? Have they been on the frontlines working on behalf of working people? Have they been carrying the laboring oar to open up opportunity for more people? Now, there are people like Bernie Sanders who I think genuinely deserved the title, because he has been in the vineyards fighting on behalf of these issues.

Obama's understanding of populism contrasts with those of the former World Bank economist Martin Wolf (2017), who wrote that "populism is an enemy of good government and even of democracy." He argued that "it may destroy independent institutions, undermine civil peace, promote xenophobia and lead to dictatorship." This is a classic example of a "bad faith" argument (Sartre 1943). It is convenient for commentators who benefit from the status quo to delegitimize challenges to it by asserting an inescapable nastiness in the counterforce. The key elements of populism – aspirations for solidarity of the political community, popular (democratic) sovereignty, widely shared economic benefits, and responsive (uncorrupted) institutions – can be inclusive. The artwork of the left-wing artist Ben Shahn captured these sentiments in his famous portraits of American workers – both black and white – urging them to use their vote "for full employment" and to "break reaction's grip."

Pippa Norris and Ronald Inglehart (2018) argue that populism is a battle between "nativism" and "cosmopolitanism," but there is no inherent democratic content to either of these concepts. In framing populism as a struggle between people who view themselves as world citizens versus those who see themselves as national citizens, Norris and Inglehart shift the discussion from the historic terrain of populism: democratic reform. Populism is not inherently a threat to democracy. It can be an opportunity to enrich, widen, and expand democracy. Populism shines light on the weakness, corruption, and unrepresentativeness of existing political institutions. It is the rallying cry of the excluded. In systems where the structures of the political system give an unfair advantage to an elite minority, as the structures of the US Constitution do, then it is not only appropriate but also essential for there to be a robust, multiracial populism to counteract them.

Taking Institutions Seriously

Multiracial populism, rather than racially polarized partisanship, is one part of the solution to the end of the Second Reconstruction. Activists needed to take political institutions seriously and learn from the missteps of reformers in both Reconstructions. The US Constitution is poisoned by undemocratic institutions, which give a leg up to the forces of white supremacy: the Supreme Court, the grossly malapportioned Senate, federalism, and the electoral college. Each of these must be attacked squarely in order to democratize the United States fully.

First, the Supreme Court must be confronted. The failure to reduce the court's power is the key institutional failure of both the First and the Second Reconstruction. The Supreme Court's power can be reduced in two ways. The first can be achieved informally by an actual or threatened court-packing plan. There is no constitutional limit on the number of justices on the court, and a president with a sympathetic Senate could theoretically appoint justices until there was a majority in favor of civil rights. We've seen this threat of "packing" institutions on a couple of occasions where democratic power was used to defeat judicial oligarchy. The most pertinent is Franklin Roosevelt's threat to appoint more justices until the Supreme Court stopped striking down New Deal legislation. A similar principle was deployed in Britain in the early twentieth century to reduce the power of the unelected House of Lords. The prime minister threatened to appoint more sympathetic peers until the Lords succumbed to the will of the Commons. Concurrently or alternatively, Congress could use its impeachment powers to remove justices who act as a brake on democratization.

A second path would be to limit formally the Supreme Court's power in the American political system. In this reform, the supremacy of judicial review would be called into question. The Constitution is not at all clear about the extent of the Supreme Court's power. Article III of the Constitution is brief and ambiguous. In the relevant passage, it simply states: "The judicial power of the United States shall be vested in one supreme court." The Constitution does not clarify what "the judicial power" means, but since the early nineteenth century, justices have asserted that it means they can strike down any law that they see as being inconsistent with the language of the Constitution, as they interpret it. This is enormous power vested in a body of appointed elites who do not face popular pressure.

Mark Tushnet (1999) argues that the American public have become excessively reliant on the courts to protect their liberties. In reality, the court is just one legitimate interpreter of the Constitution. The president and Congress also have a duty to interpret the Constitution. Some might argue that removing the "final say" of the Supreme Court would lead to chaos, but there are other constitutional systems in which the judiciary does not have the "final say." In the British system, it is Parliament that has this final say and can overrule judicial proclamations with a simple majority vote. Ultimately, it is the public that has the final constitutional say in this system, because if the public does not agree with Parliament's constitutional reform, the MPs who voted for it can be removed at the next election. If Congress disagrees with the court, Congress should be able to overturn a court decision.

This kind of democratic responsiveness, however, depends on political power emerging from a system of "one person, one vote." There are currently two major violations to this principle in the US federal system: (1) the electoral college and (2) Senate malapportionment. The electoral college should be scrapped, but a constitutional amendment to abolish it would be difficult. Constitutional amendments, according to Article V, require support from two-thirds of Congress and three-quarters of states. Low-population states are given excessive advantage in this process, making any effort to pass a centralizing constitutional amendment challenging. The Fourteenth Amendment, which helped to centralize power and nationalize rights in the 1860s, was only made possible because Congress was able to use the Union victory in the Civil War as a means of compelling the defeated South to ratify the amendment.

There is a way to destroy the electoral college without constitutional amendment. Since 2007, an effort has been under way for states to bypass the Article V requirements of congressional and state-legislative supermajorities. The National Popular Vote Interstate Compact takes advantage of the decentralized nature of the US electoral system for a more popular, majoritarian aim. The Constitution allows states to allocate their electoral votes as they see fit. Forty-eight states give all their electoral votes to the statewide popular vote winner. Two states (Maine and Nebraska) allocate two electoral votes to their state's popular vote winner and then each remaining electoral vote is allocated according to the number of congressional districts a candidate won in the state. For example, in 2016 Hillary Clinton won the state of Maine overall, but lost its Second District to Donald Trump. Clinton was awarded three electoral votes, while Donald Trump was allocated one. In the past, electoral votes have been allocated through other means, including by taking the vote away from the public entirely and handing it to state legislatures.

The National Popular Vote Interstate Compact proposes that states allocate their electoral votes in a new way: according to the winner of the *national* popular vote, irrespective of who won their state. Under this scenario, a state like California would have awarded its 55 electoral votes to George W. Bush in 2004, in spite of the state itself voting for John Kerry, because Bush won the national popular vote (on that occasion). Texas would have given its 38 electoral votes to Hillary Clinton in 2016. The compact does not go into effect until states totaling an electoral college majority (270) agree to participate. Sixteen states have currently signed up, totaling 196 electoral votes.

Senate malapportionment is one of the most troubling, yet intractable undemocratic features of the US Constitution. The Senate's complete disregard for population differences between its constituencies and its relative strength within the American federal system is unique in the United States and rare internationally, even among federal systems. Yet, scholars have largely overlooked its political consequences. These consequences are extremely important, however, as these structures tilt the rules of the political game to favor certain groups of voters over others. The midterm elections in 2018 – in which Democrats received 12.8 million more votes than the Republicans, but still lost senators – show how strongly Republicans are current beneficiaries of Senate malapportionment.

Deviation from the principle of "one person, one vote" through the equal representation of states in the US Senate is often defended with reference to protections for "the minority" from the "the majority." This view, although widespread, is deeply problematic because it wrongly assumes that all minorities are protected by equal state apportionment. While some groups do benefit from equal state apportionment (namely, the minority of Americans who live in low-population states without major urban areas), other minority groups – urban dwellers and, especially, racial minorities – are underrepresented as a result of equal state representation.

Equal representation in the Senate has two additional consequences that have substantial implications for American democratic politics. First, current Senate apportionment weakens the democratic link between policy commitment and delivery. For entirely arbitrary reasons, presidents are blocked from gaining passage of preferred legislation, which would have otherwise passed. The electorate votes for policy changes, sometimes with very strong majorities, at both congressional and presidential levels, only to see these initiatives fall due to the Senate's obsolete institutional configuration. Over time, the inability for people to see the change for which they voted can undermine democratic legitimacy and trust in government.

Second, the principle of one person, one vote is widely understood to be a keystone of representative democracies. While some federal countries allow for departure from this principle to account for territorial representation in places where territories represent at-risk ethnic or religious minorities, as a general matter, such deviations are fundamentally anti-majoritarian and will *ipso facto* diminish the representation of people in more populous parts of the country.

Understanding who these citizens are is crucial to our understanding of which groups of citizens benefit most from the existing rules of the game. Under equal state representation, white Americans are the winners, whereas African Americans and Hispanics receive diminished representation (see Figure 5.2).

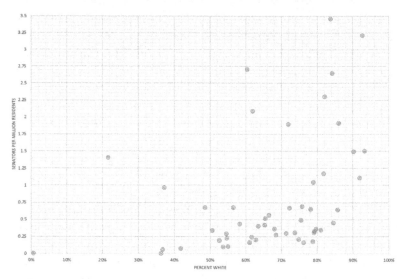

Population data are from the American Communities Survey 2017, US Census Bureau; Puerto Rico and the District of Columbia are included and score "0" on the y-axis
Figure 5.2: Senators per million residents, sorted by percent of residents who are white

Equal representation in the Senate is protected by Article V of the US Constitution, which says "that no state, without its consent, shall be deprived of its equal suffrage in the Senate." Some, therefore, might argue that it is just a fact of life of American politics – not worth mentioning. But this leaves a potentially major source of gridlock and voter frustration unexamined. Irrespective of the practical likelihood of reapportioning the Senate on a different basis, Americans should nonetheless be aware of its effects, including whom it advantages and disadvantages.

Even though the Senate cannot be easily reapportioned, its pivotal place in the American lawmaking process could be readjusted. The Senate has an unusual amount of power for an upper chamber, and it is even possible that a constitutional amendment equivalent to the "Parliament Act" in the United Kingdom could substantially diminish the

Senate's ability to block legislation approved in the House of Representatives. The Parliament Act was a twentieth-century constitutional reform in the United Kingdom that removed the upper chamber's ability to block permanently legislation approved in the popularly elected lower house. There is no reason why the US Constitution could not be amended to create a similar arrangement in America's bicameral system.

There are other reforms that could help to democratize the United States further, which do not need a constitutional amendment. To balance modestly the overrepresentation of rural, overwhelmingly white states, statehood could be given to the District of Columbia, which has a population larger than two states (Vermont and Wyoming), and to Puerto Rico, which has more than three million American citizens who also have no representation in the Senate. These jurisdictions are also majority non-white. In the First Reconstruction, Republicans used Congress's power to add states to the union to help bolster their partisan pro-civil rights majority. The Radical Republican Congress even added Nebraska as a state in defiance of President Andrew Johnson's veto. Today's Democrats should not hesitate to do the same for the District of Columbia or Puerto Rico. The former is especially disadvantaged because, although it pays greater total levels of income tax than twenty-two states, it has no voting representation in the Congress that writes the legislation that taxes its residents.

Conclusion

During the First Reconstruction, resistance to democratic backsliding persisted for decades after the removal of federal troops. State-level efforts kept glimmers of multiracial democracy alive for a generation after the federal government abandoned its policy of "forceful federalism" for civil rights. Ultimately, however, state-level resistance is inadequate. Failure by the federal government to provide legal – and, indeed, physical – protection to pro-Reconstruction political activists ultimately spelled their undoing.

Three decades of federal inaction, coupled with state-level fraud, violence, and intimidation, eradicated all the reforms of the First Reconstruction.

While states might attempt to act as a bulwark against the end of the Second Reconstruction, it is unlikely that they can prevail for long without federal backing. The history of civil rights and multiracial inclusion has shown that it depends on sustained federal commitment. The full coercive power of the national government has always been required to stamp out white supremacist terrorism. In its absence, the United States faces a crisis of civil rights.

Conclusion

If the policy of the Government upon vital questions affecting the whole people is to be irrevocably fixed by decisions of the Supreme Court ... the people will have ceased to be their own rulers, having to that extent practically resigned their Government into the hands of that eminent tribunal.

Abraham Lincoln, First Inaugural Address (1861)

The rise and fall of the two Reconstructions lay waste to blithe narratives of American exceptionalism. Both Reconstructions complicate conventional, linear accounts of US political development. Scholars have long portrayed American democracy as existing on a steady conveyor belt to ever-greater freedom (Hartz 1955; Myrdal 1944; Lipset 1963; Huntington 1981). Even recent commentaries have denied democratic backsliding in the United States. Daron Acemoglu and James Robinson write in their widely cited book that "the United States experienced a gradual movement toward democracy with no reverses" (2005: xi). This claim is utterly incompatible with the history of Reconstruction. The United States has experienced one very serious, clear-cut case of democratic reversal. In this book, I argue that it is currently experiencing a second.

Both Reconstructions should puncture inflated claims that the United States was founded on ideas of equality, inclusion, and democratic citizenship. Writers are wrong to say that the American War of Independence constituted "the world's first democratic revolution," which aimed "to break with patterns of elite rule altogether" (Gerstle 2015: 17). The American Revolution was fought, in large part, to protect institutions that were fundamentally undemocratic, not the least of which was slavery (Horne 2014; Johnson 2016). Southern plantation owners were keen supporters of the American Revolution, fearful that the British Parliament would abolish slavery in the Empire without their consent (Van Cleve 2010). The House of Lords ruled slavery unlawful in Britain in 1772, three years before the first battle of the War of Independence.[1] A Parliament that could impose taxes without the consent of colonial legislatures could also impose the abolition of slavery.

It was not an unfounded fear, given that Parliament did precisely that in 1833 with the Slavery Abolition Act. Had America not won its independence and remained within the British Empire, the legislation would have ended slavery in the American South three decades earlier than it did, with enormous consequences for American social and political development. It is no coincidence that some of the most enthusiastic protagonists of American independence were the slaveholding elite. The first president, George Washington, owned more than three hundred slaves; the author of the Declaration of Independence, Thomas Jefferson, enslaved six hundred people; the main author of the US Constitution, James Madison, held more than one hundred slaves. Keri Leigh Merritt (2017) estimates that a person who owned more than ten slaves would be in the wealthiest 1 percent of southern residents. Those who owned more than five hundred slaves would constitute the top 0.01 percent – the billionaire class of their day.

George III also attracted ire for the Proclamation of 1763, which forbade settlement west of the Appalachian Mountains by white British subjects. The measure was designed to protect Native Americans, who were given exclusive right to inhabit the lands between the Appalachian Mountains and the Mississippi River. This directive was regarded as an act of appalling tyranny by white Americans who wished to push westward and strip the Native Americans of the fertile Ohio River Valley territory. A less popularly quoted passage in the Declaration of Independence is Thomas Jefferson's racist rant against George III for failing to deploy British troops to exterminate the Native Americans in this territory. The Declaration denounces the King who "has endeavored to bring on the inhabitants of our frontiers the merciless Indian savages, whose known rule of warfare is undistinguished destruction of all ages, sexes, and conditions."

Some commentators acknowledge these practical shortcomings, but argue that the United States was founded on noble principles of liberty, democracy, and equality. Gary Gerstle, for example, credits the United States with "democratic, liberal, and federal beginnings" (2015: 1). Philip Gleason argues that "exclusiveness ran contrary to the logic of the defining principles, and the official commitment to those principles has worked historically to overcome and to make the practical boundaries of American identity with its theoretical universalism" (1980: 62–3).

Evidence for "official commitment" to the principles of "theoretical universalism" is unpersuasive. Slaveholding elites constituted the main authors of the Declaration of Independence and the US Constitution. They made up the majority of America's founding presidents. At the end of the American Revolution, in the Treaty of Paris (1783) negotiations, the US government demanded the return of American slaves who had fled during the war.[2]

The US Constitution strengthened and protected the institution of slavery.[3] Section 4 of the Constitution created a nationwide anti-fugitive slave regime. It authorized the federal government to overrule state laws or individuals who tried to protect runaway slaves and free blacks. This section was given statutory effect by Congress and signed into law by George Washington in 1793.[4] Under the Fugitive Slave

Act of 1793, anyone who gave shelter or assistance to an escaped slave – or merely failed to report knowledge about their existence – would be liable for a fine of $500 (per capita annual income in 1790 was $498). The act was even more pernicious in that children who were born to escaped slaves in free territory were also considered the property of their mother's owner for the rest of their lives. They, too, could be captured and enslaved, in spite of being born in a free state. There was a certain irony that in the same year that the US Congress passed this act, the colonial legislature of Upper Canada, which refused to sign up to the Declaration of Independence, abolished slavery.

The official commitment of the US government was not to "theoretical universalism." It was committed to racially restricted citizenship. The notion that American meant "white" was pervasive, not just in the South, but across the entire country. In the antebellum period, even "free" blacks were viewed as un-American. David Bateman (2018) has meticulously chronicled that when white northerners had the chance, they more often than not deprived African Americans of equal citizenship. Abraham Lincoln was a long-time supporter of deporting freed slaves to Africa, believing that they could never fully become American. Psychological studies today confirm that many Americans still associate American nationality as "implicitly synonymous with being white" (Devos and Banaji 2005).

The Supreme Court spent more than half of its history insisting on the inherent whiteness of American citizenship. In the antebellum period, the court denied that a black person could be a US citizen, ruling that "a free negro of the African race, whose ancestors were brought to this country and sold as slaves, is not a 'citizen' within the meaning of the Constitution of the United States" (*Dred Scott v. Sandford*, 1857). In *Elk v. Wilkins* (1884) the court denied citizenship to Native Americans. In the twentieth century, the court repeatedly denied US citizenship to Asian people (*Ozawa v. US*, 1922; *US v. Thind*, 1923). It authorized the locking up of Japanese Americans who had committed no crime, including children (*Korematsu v. US*, 1944). It has recently given legal sanction to blanket bans on arrivals to the United States from countries whose only crime seems to be that they are populated by Muslim majorities (*Trump v. Hawaii*, 2018).

Racial exclusion is not contrary to the defining principles of the American project. It *was* the defining principle of American citizenship and would have remained so had it not been violently challenged in the most destructive conflict the United States has ever experienced. About 750,000 men died in the Civil War – more than all America's other military adventures, before or since, combined. Showing the huge human, fiscal, and economic costs of the war, 20 percent of the Mississippi state budget in 1866 was spent on buying artificial limbs for ex-solders (White 2017:28). As of 2019, the US federal government is still paying a monthly pension to the child of a Union veteran.

It is this revolution – in which slaves and radicals were the victors – in which Americans should take pride, not the revolt of the 1770s led by wealthy coastal merchants opposed to customs duties, slaveowners fearing abolition, and rapacious white settlers hungering after indigenous lands. Josiah Walls, Fredrick Douglass, and Thaddeus Stevens should be the revolutionary heroes about whom American children learn, not Washington, Jefferson, and Madison.

Similarly, the civil rights movement of the mid-twentieth century should not be regarded as simply part of a conveyor belt of democratization. It was fiercely – and in some cases brutally – resisted. Between the two Reconstructions, violent resistance to democracy in America did not go away. It took federal occupation of the South, once more, to guarantee equal citizenship rights. These comparisons have been made before and in excellent scholarship (Kousser 1999; Valelly 2004; Berman 2015). This book adds to these works by arguing that the United States is currently undergoing a reversal of the Second Reconstruction. The lessons of the failure of the First Reconstruction are pertinent to under-standing the collapse of the Second.

Skeptics of this argument might be rankled. How could a country that has twice elected a black president, with thousands of non-white elected officials, possibly go into reverse, along racial lines, and become a non-democratic state? They might point out that the Constitution guarantees "equal protection of the law," and that it is protected by modern legislation such as the Civil Rights Act of 1964 and the Voting Rights Act of 1965.

Something similar could have been asked in the early 1870s. Who could possibly have foreseen the impending, total democratic backsliding in a country that had twice elected a heroic, pro-civil rights Union general, who owed his victory to the mass mobilization of black voters, with a multiracial Congress and thousands of African Americans in public office, with new state constitutions and constitutional amendments guaranteeing equality under the law? Few Americans during the First Reconstruction knew its collapse would come; it was easy to assume progress was inevitable. This book warns against making the same mistake in the twilight of the Second Reconstruction.

This is not to say that there are no differences between the two Reconstructions. There are many. The Second Reconstruction is undoubtedly further reaching, more inclusive, and more embedded. The Second Reconstruction did genuinely have cross-party and broad acceptance – at least for a period of time – in the way that the First Reconstruction never did. The First Reconstruction was always built on somewhat shallow foundations, far more so than the Second Reconstruction. There has been some broad cultural and attitudinal progress among whites, which did not happen to the same extent in the nineteenth century. But, there is no particular reason to think that the Second Reconstruction is destined to endure indefinitely.

The Ku Klux Klan are not blowing up school buses today, but they do not need to do so. After the collapse of the Democratic Party in the South and Midwest during the Obama presidency, new Republican state legislatures legalized devices, such as school district secession, to facilitate school segregation (Johnson and King 2019). Schools in the United States no longer have "white only" signs above them, but in parts of the country they have achieved the same function through less detectable means. The racial homogeneity of American schools today resembles that of fifty years ago. For many black and Hispanic students, their monoracial school environments make it seem as if *Brown v. Board of Education* never happened.

The end of democracy in the United States may not come in the form in which we typically see democratic reversals on television. There probably won't be a military general rolling down Pennsylvania Avenue in a tank wearing aviator sunglasses and a beret. America's formal institutions could well persist, even after multiracial democracy has collapsed. Congress might not be dissolved; the American flag might continue to fly over public buildings; elections might not be cancelled.

What is likely to happen is that, while familiar institutions might endure in a formal sense, their democratic character will fade. Congress will continue to meet, but it will be elected by a shrunken electorate, representing constituencies that violate all basic understandings of the principle of "one person, one vote," either through extreme partisan gerrymandering or Senate malapportionment. The balance of power may increasingly shift away from democratically elected officials to actors without democratic accountability: a Senate made up of "rotten boroughs," a White House perennially occupied by popular vote losers, an all-powerful Supreme Court packed with hostile actors, appointed by presidents who lack popular support and confirmed by senators who represent a minority of the country. State governments will use their wide-ranging local powers to rewrite the rules of the political game to secure single-party rule in perpetuity and with impunity. The United States is already well on its way down this path.

Notes

Introduction

1 "Circulars Call for Ostracism of Meredith," *Greenville Delta Democrat-Times*, November 8, 1962.
2 "Dark Clouds," *Hattiesburg American*, October 2, 1962.
3 "Meredith Hanged in Effigy," *Greenwood Commonwealth*, September 14, 1962.
4 Native Americans on reservations did not get the right to vote in Arizona, New Mexico, Idaho, Maine, Mississippi, or Washington until the 1940s. They did not get the right to vote in Utah until 1957 or in Colorado until 1970. Alaska banned Native Alaskans who were not proficient in English from voting until the 1970s (National Commission on Voting Rights, 2014).
5 The Twenty-Third Amendment extended the right to vote in presidential elections to the citizens of Washington, DC (who were predominantly black). The Twenty-Fourth Amendment prohibited the poll tax, which had been used to block African Americans from voting.
6 Adie Ball in Alabama and Minnie Cox in Mississippi. Both were postmistresses, a party patronage post appointed directly by the president. A key emissary of the national party outside Washington, their "party" roles included using their office to distribute campaign material, being a local ear for the party,

and raising money by selling a party newspaper or other items on the side. As George Mayer (1964) wrote in his classic history of the Republican Party, "[the postmaster's] negative power to withhold information was almost as important as his power to issue it. Pamphlets mailed by the opposition party often wound up in waste baskets instead of post boxes."

Chapter 1   The Rise of the First Reconstruction

1   Karl Marx complained in a letter to Friedrich Engels in August 1862 that the Union war effort had hitherto "been dominated by the representatives of the border slave states." But Marx believed that the Union Army would soon be transformed into an anti-slavery force. A month before Lincoln issued the Emancipation Proclamation, Marx predicted: "In my view, all this is going to take another turn. The North will, at last, wage the war in earnest, have recourse to revolutionary methods [e.g., abolition of slavery and black soldiers] and overthrow the supremacy of the border slave statesmen. One single nigger regiment would have a remarkable effect on Southern nerves" (Marx to Engels, August 7, 1862).

2   Karl Marx spectacularly misjudged Johnson. In a letter to Engels, he wrote hastily: "Lincoln's assassination was the most stupid act they [pro-slavery whites] could have committed. Johnson is stern, inflexible, revengeful, and as a former poor White has a deadly hatred of the oligarchy. He will make less fuss about these fellows, and, because of the treachery, he will find the temper of the North commensurate with his intentions" (Marx to Engels, May 1, 1865).

3   The United States' most significant export in the mid-nineteenth century was cotton. The disruption of cotton production during the Civil War was not only enough to devastate the southern economy, but also brought economic ruin and even famine to America's international export markets (Longmate 1978).

4   Karl Marx understood the materialist implications. In *Capital*, he wrote: "Mr Wade, vice-president of the United States [i.e., Benjamin Wade, Senate president pro tempore], declared in public meetings that, after the abolition of slavery, a radical change of the relations of capital and of property in land is next upon the order of the day" (1887 [1867]: xx).

5 Typical of this blindness, *Nation* magazine, the mouthpiece of twentieth-century American liberalism, belittled W. E. B. Du Bois for portraying slaves as agents of their own economic emancipation. The magazine's review of Du Bois's scholarship was withering: "Du Bois's race consciousness distorts his Marxism; so that the net result of *Black Reconstruction* is to add more confusion than light to one of the most crucial epochs of American history. The Negro masses did not play a conscious and decisive role in their own emancipation" (Spero 1935: 108).

6 https://timesmachine.nytimes.com/timesmachine/1868/09/12/78955747.pdf.

7 Thaddeus Stevens, speech to the citizens of Lancaster, September 6, 1865.

8 Congressional Republicans sought to inflate the pro-Union numbers by adding three new states in the 1860s (West Virginia, Nevada, and Nebraska). The addition of Nevada was especially dubious, given that this state, with only 6,857 residents, would be afforded the same number of senators as states like New York (population 3.8 million) and Pennsylvania (population 2.9 million).

9 Author's calculations based on Department of Defense data ("selected Manpower Statistics," Department of Defense Report, Directorate for Information Operations and Reports [DIOR], Fiscal Year 1997).

10 Andrew Johnson, State of the Union Address, December 9, 1868.

11 "Alabama," *Chicago Daily Tribune*, October 14, 1878.

12 Josiah Walls, speech in the US House of Representatives, February 3, 1872.

13 Thaddeus Stevens, speech to the citizens of Lancaster, September 6, 1865.

Chapter 2   The Fall of the First Reconstruction

1 Craig Waters, "Where is Josiah T Wall [*sic*], Florida's first black Congressman," *Tallahassee Democrat*, February 27, 2018.

2 *Florida Times Union*, September 14, 1884.

3 Speech by Congressman Josiah Walls to the US House of Representatives, February 3, 1872.

4 Speech by Congressman Josiah Walls to the US House of Representatives, February 3, 1872.
5 Speech by Congressman Josiah Walls to the US House of Representatives, 1874.
6 Party and bureaucracy have been (and remain) intimately linked in the USA. In the nineteenth century, postmasterships were the most widespread form of such party patronage, accounting for two-thirds of the federal jobs that the president could appoint directly. About eighty African Americans were appointed postmasters and customs officials during Reconstruction (Foner 1993).
7 Charles Francis Adams, "The Solid South and the Afro-American Race Problem," speech delivered to the Academy of Music (Richmond, VA), October 24, 1908.
8 Letter from W. H. Taft to N. W. Aldrich, January 31, 1909.
9 Letter from W. H. Taft to W. R. Nelson, February 23, 1909.
10 Letter from T. Roosevelt to W. H. Taft, February 26, 1909.
11 But even this contribution has been exaggerated (Chemerinsky 2014).
12 This ruling blocking a federal income tax was overturned by the Sixteenth Amendment in 1913.
13 One might draw a parallel with the Supreme Court's convenient "switch" in favor of the New Deal after Franklin Roosevelt won a huge majority in Congress in the 1936 election. Roosevelt's threat to force recalcitrant judges to retire and to pack the court with pro-New Deal appointees resulted in the famous "switch in time which saved nine" (*West Coast Hotel v. Parrish*, 1937).
14 What might have also been at issue was that the state of Louisiana required these publicly owned abattoirs to be racially integrated.
15 "Parish" is the Louisiana term for "county."
16 An informational sign outside the new courthouse still presents the event as a "riot" rather than a massacre, and celebrates it as having led to an "end of carpetbag misrule in the South" – a reference to the legitimately elected black Republicans and their white allies.
17 "Colonel Whitley's View," *Emporia Gazette*, March 26, 1906.
18 *Alabama State Journal*, December 4, 1869.
19 *Mobile Register*, November 4, 1874.
20 In the 1910s–30s, unions affiliated to the Communist Party

returned to the southern fields to unionize black share-croppers. In the 1930s, the Sharecroppers Union (SCU) distributed literature to sharecroppers in Tallapoosa County, Alabama, informing them that they had a right to sell their own crops, grow their own food, get paid at least a dollar a day, and send their children to school. They began to sign up members, but local law enforcement responded by arresting dozens of union members on trumped-up charges. The body of one union member was dumped on the steps of the county courthouse. In Dallas County, Alabama, the SCU's organizers were arrested and delivered at gunpoint by the sheriff to a white mob, which drove the union reps to the outskirts of Selma, stripped them naked, tied them to trees, whipped them with horsewhips, and then set their wounds on fire (Forner 2017: Ch. 3).

21 Frederick Douglass, "Letter to Private Dalzell," October 3, 1883.

22 During the interview, in May 2014, Brooke recalled his grandfather fondly: "I was very close to him. He was an interesting man. Dark color and wide eyes. Straight black hair. So you could see the Indian [heritage], which was quite beautiful. He was very jovial and whatnot. He himself I think was educated by the slave masters. They must have taken to him and seen that he had potential and he was bright."

23 In 1878, Republican President Hayes signed the Democrats' Posse Comitatus Act into law, which prohibited the United States Marshals from summoning troops to suppress white supremacist violence, tying his own hands (or washing them) of responsibility for protecting black civil rights using coercive force.

24 Literacy tests were designed with questions that had highly subjective or even impossible answers (e.g., "Who is an elector?"), leaving it to the discretion of local registrars to interpret whether an applicant had provided a "correct" answer. Invariably, the local, white Democratic registrars would approve white responses, while marking down black responses. Grandfather clauses exempted descendents of those who were able to vote before a certain date (always set before the Thirteenth Amendment) from barriers such as literacy tests or poll taxes.

Chapter 3   The Rise of the Second Reconstruction

1   "Editorials," *The Crisis*, July 1946.
2   Paul Mayhew, "The Talmadge Story," *The New Republic*, July 23, 1956.
3   "Lynchings," *The Boston Globe*, July 27, 1946; "America's Last Mass Lynching is a Cold Case," *Washington Post*, October 24, 2019; "Grand Jury Sifts Lynching Evidence," *Chattanooga Daily Times*, December 4, 1946.
4   Moorfield Storey, "The Negro Question: An Address Delivered before the Wisconsin Bar Association," June 27, 1918.
5   Megan Francis (2014) argues that this shift by the court had occurred two decades earlier in *Moore v. Dempsey* (1923), a case about race-baiting mobs in courtrooms. While *Moore* did involve the Supreme Court intervening in a state criminal case on behalf of black defendants, its importance should not be overstated. The court only intervened in the 1920s and 1930s in cases of "flagrant injustices" (e.g., torture, disorderly mobs in courtrooms). Michael Klarman argues that "none of these rulings had a very significant direct impact on Jim Crow Justice" (2000: 49). Gunnar Myrdal records that even racist whites who opposed integration or black enfranchisement balked at blatantly unfair criminal trials against obviously innocent black defendants (1944: 60–1). Indeed, after the court's ruling in *Moore*, the Arkansas Democratic governor Thomas McRae commuted the defendants' sentences.
6   Ta-Nehisi Coates, "The Case for Reparations," *The Atlantic*, June 2014.
7   O. John Rogge (assistant attorney general) to all US attorneys, memo accompanying Circular Number 3356, Supplement I, May 21, 1940.
8   175,895 African Americans fought in the Union Army; the free black population of males aged 15–40 in the non-Confederate states in the 1860 Census was 90,954. This means that a majority of black soldiers in the Union Army were liberated slaves.
9   Christopher Thorne (1974) writes about the awkwardness of US troop segregation in Britain, where many segregated units were stationed.
10 In a similar vein, Vice-President Richard Nixon (1957) wrote a memo to President Dwight Eisenhower after a trip to Ghana:

"We cannot talk equality to the peoples of Africa and Asia and practice inequality in the United States. In the national interest, as well as for the moral issues involved, we must support the necessary steps which will assure orderly progress in the elimination of discrimination in the United States."

11 Harry Truman, "Special Message to Congress on Civil Rights," February 2, 1948 (Washington, DC).

12 Hubert Humphrey, speech to the Democratic National Convention, July 14, 1948 (Philadelphia, PA).

13 Although *Brown* was decided after Truman left office, Truman's Department of Justice had been involved in the case since 1952 and filed a supportive *amicus curiae* brief.

14 "We Will Not Surrender," *Selma Times-Journal*, 26 September, 1957.

15 J. Fred Thornton, "A New Curtain Rises on New Reconstruction," *Montgomery Advertiser*, October 3, 1957.

16 Personal interview with Edward Brooke, May 3, 2014 (Coral Gables, FL).

17 Mary McGrory, "Voting Rights Makes Strange Bedfellows," *Washington Post*, May 9, 1982.

18 However, Ackerman (2014: Ch 6) argues that Section 10 of the Voting Rights Act was more important than the Twenty-Fourth Amendment in achieving this goal.

19 Personal interview with Edward Brooke, 4 May, 2014 (Coral Gables, FL).

20 Letter from Edward Brooke to Martin Luther King, April 1, 1968, Box 197, Edward Brooke Papers (Library of Congress, Washington, DC).

21 Jesse Helms, quoted in "Racial Themes Arise in Senate Campaign," *Raleigh News and Observer*, November 1, 1990.

22 Gantt, interview with UNCTV, 2016.

23 Personal interview with Letetia Daniels Jackson (by phone), December 9, 2013.

24 Personal interview with Monty Halger (by phone), November 20, 2013.

25 Lyndon Johnson, "Remarks on the Signing of the Voting Rights Act," August 6, 1965.

26 Ulysses Grant, "Special Message to Congress," March 30, 1870.

27 *Montgomery Advertiser*, March 17, 1965.

28 *Montgomery Advertiser*, August 9–10, 1965.

29 Jackson won 13 percent of the white Democratic primary vote in his 1988 presidential campaign (Tate 1994. 12).

Chapter 4 The Compromise of 2016

1 In 1974, the Democrats gained 628 seats; in 2010, the Republicans gained 680 seats.
2 Proceedings of the Constitutional Convention of the State of Alabama, May 22, 1901, p. 15.
3 Jason Zengerle, "The New Racism," *The New Republic*, August 2014.
4 Fred Barnes, "The Crimson Tide," *The Weekly Standard*, November 22, 2010.
5 Benjamin Harrison, "Proclamation on the Death of Ex-President Hayes," January 18, 1893.
6 Pew Research Center, *The Partisan Divide on Political Values Grows Even Wider*, October 5, 2017. https://www.people-press.org/wp-content/uploads/sites/4/2017/10/10-05-2017-Political-landscape-release-updt..pdf.
7 See www.undocs.org/A/HRC/38/33/ADD.1.
8 James Vardaman, *Greenwood Commonwealth*, August 17, 1900.
9 "No to Medicaid Expansion, Despite Strong Citizen Support," *Jackson Free Press*, January 15, 2019.

Chapter 5 Reconstructing Reconstruction

1 Carol Moseley Braun, "Between W. E. B. Du Bois and B. T. Washington," *Ebony*, November 1995.
2 Ibid.
3 Gretchen Reynolds, "Behind the Braun Phenomenon," *Chicago Tribune*, October 1992.
4 The choice of attempting to desegregate a beach was an especially powerful move given that the Chicago Race Riot of 1919, the worst in the state's history, was sparked by the murder of a black swimmer on a white-only beach.
5 Personal interview with Carol Moseley Braun (Chicago, August 22, 2013).
6 Personal interviews with Jim Charlton (Chicago, August 26, 2013) and Ira Cohen (Chicago, August 27, 2013).

7   Personal interview with Carol Moseley Braun (Chicago, April 15, 2015).
8   "Black Power and the Civil Rights Crisis," *Negro Digest*, December 1966.
9   Personal interview with Carol Moseley Braun (Chicago, April 15, 2015).
10 Personal interview with Alton Miller, August 27, 2013.
11 "Braun Takes Heat on Funds," *Chicago Sun-Times*, October 1, 1992. Braun's full quote is: "The same people who attempted to peddle racism in this campaign found that it wasn't going to be bought by the people of Illinois, and now they are trying to manufacture a scandal."
12 Personal interview with Carol Moseley Braun (Chicago, April 15, 2015).
13 Personal interview with Heather Booth, September 13, 2013.
14 Personal interview with Carol Moseley Braun (Chicago, August 22, 2013).
15 *Virginia Sun*, May 25, 1892.

Conclusion

1   *Somerset v. Stewart* (1772) found slavery unlawful in England and Wales; *Knight v. Wedderburn* (1778) found slavery unlawful in Scotland.
2   The British government refused to honor this request.
3   The Bill of Rights did not, as Gerstle claims, "pioneer new thinking about personhood and inviolability." It codified many longstanding ancient English and Scottish rights that had hitherto been held as conventional under the uncodified British constitution. The authors of the American Bill of Rights were not radicals: they were conservatives.
4   Washington used the law to pursue one of his own slaves, Oney Judge, who escaped from the President's Mansion in 1796. Initially, the Washingtons assumed she must have been kidnapped by "a Frenchman," there having been "no suspicion of her going off or provocation to do so." Years later, Judge told an interviewer that she had a very real provocation to go: Washington was not re-standing for election that year, which meant she would soon be returned to the brutality of plantation slavery in Virginia.

References

Acemoglu, Daron, and James Robinson. 2005. *The Economic Origins of Democracy and Dictatorship*. Cambridge: Cambridge University Press.

Ackerman, Bruce. 2014. *We the People, Volume 3: The Civil Rights Revolution*. Cambridge, MA: Harvard University Press.

Alexander, Michelle. 2012. *The New Jim Crow*. New York: The New Press.

Allen, Jonathan, and Amie Parnes. 2017. *Shattered: Inside Hillary Clinton's Doomed Campaign*. New York: Crown.

Anderson, Eric. 1981. *Race and Politics in North Carolina, 1872–1901*. Baton Rouge: Louisiana State University Press.

Archarya, Avidit, Matthew Blackwell, and Maya Sen. 2018. *Deep Roots: How Slavery Still Shapes Southern Politics*. Princeton, NJ: Princeton University Press.

Axelrod, David. 2015: *Believer: My Forty Years in Politics*. New York: Penguin Books.

Baldwin, James, and Margaret Mead. 1971. *A Rap on Race*. New York: Random House.

Banfield, Edward, and James Wilson. 1963. *City Politics*. Cambridge, MA: Harvard University Press.

Bateman, David. 2018. *Disenfranchising Democracy: Constructing the Electorate in the United States, the United Kingdom, and France*. Cambridge: Cambridge University Press.

Bateman, David. 2019. "Partisan Polarization on Black Suffrage, 1785–1868." *Perspectives on Politics*, 1–22. doi:10.1017/S1537592719001087.

Behrend, Jacqueline, and Laurence Whitehead (eds.). 2016. *Illiberal Practices: Territorial Variance within Large Federal Democracies*. Baltimore, MD: Johns Hopkins University Press.

Behrens, Angela, Christopher Uggen, and Jeff Manza. 2003. "Ballot Manipulation and the Menace of Negro Domination: Racial Threat and Felon Disenfranchisement in the United States, 1850–2002." *American Journal of Sociology* 109:3, 559–605.

Bell, Daniel (ed.). 1964. *The Radical Right*. New York: Doubleday.

Berman, Ari. 2015. *Give Us the Ballot: The Modern Struggle for Voting Rights in America*. New York: Farrar, Straus, and Giroux.

Bermeo, Nancy. 2003. *Ordinary People in Extraordinary Times: The Citizenry and the Breakdown of Democracy*. Princeton, NJ: Princeton University Press.

Bernd, Joseph. 1972. "Georgia: Static and Dynamic," in William C. Havard (ed.), *The Changing Politics of the South*. Baton Rouge: Louisiana State University Press.

Bethel, Elizabeth. 1981. *Promiseland: A Century of Life in a Negro Community*. Philadelphia, PA: Temple University Press.

Bickel, Alexander, and Benno Schmidt. 1984. *The Judiciary and Responsible Government*. New York: Macmillan.

Bleser, Carol. 1969. *The Promised Land: The History of the South Carolina Land Commission, 1869–1890*. Columbia: University of South Carolina Press.

Bonfili, David. 1998. "Single Member Districting in Theory and Practice." MLitt thesis, Faculty of Social Sciences, University of Oxford.

Bositis, David. 2004. *Blacks and the 2004 Democratic National Convention*. Washington, DC: Joint Center for Political and Economic Studies.

Bowes, Darren. 2019. "From Mansfield to Little Rock: Eisenhower and the School Desegregation Crises, 1956–1957." MA dissertation. Lancaster University.

Brooke, Edward. 1966. *The Challenge of Change*. Boston, MA: Little, Brown, & Co.

Brooke, Edward. 2007. *Bridging the Divide: My Life*. New Brunswick, NJ: Rutgers University Press.

Brooks, Noah. 1895. *Washington in Lincoln's Time*. New York: The Century Co.

Browne, Stephen. 2008. "Andrew Johnson and the Politics of Character," In Martin J. Medhurst (ed.), *Before the Rhetorical Presidency*. College Station: Texas A&M University Press.

Burke, W. Lewis. 2000. "The Radical Law School," in James Lowell Underwood and W. Lewis Burke (eds.), *At Freedom's Door: African American Founding Fathers and Lawyers in Reconstruction South Carolina*. Columbia: University of South Carolina Press.

Cannon, David. 1999. *Race, Redistricting, and Representation*. Chicago, IL: University of Chicago Press.

Cheathem, Mark. 2018. *The Coming of Democracy: Presidential Campaigning in the Age of Jackson*. Baltimore, MD: Johns Hopkins University Press.

Chereminsky, Erwin. 2014. *The Case Against the Supreme Court*. New York: Viking.

Chestnut, J. L. 2007. *Black in Selma*. Tuscaloosa: University of Alabama Press.

Chin, Gabriel. 2002. "Rehabilitating Unconstitutional Statutes." *University of Cincinnati Law Review* 71, 421–455.

Christensen, Matthew. 2012. "The St. Landry Massacre: Reconstruction's Deadliest Episode of Violence." MA thesis. Milwaukee: University of Wisconsin.

Coulter, E. Merton. 1947. *The South During Reconstruction*. Baton Rouge: Louisiana State University Press.

Crowe, Justin. 2010. "Westward Expansion, Preapportionment Politics, and the Making of the Southern Supreme Court." *Studies in American Political Development* 24, 90–120.

Cushman, Clare. 2013. *Supreme Court Justices*. London: Sage.

Cutler, John Henry. 1972. *Ed Brooke: Biography of a Senator*. Indianapolis, IN: Bobbs-Merrill Company.

Daniell, Elizabeth. 1975. "The Ashburn Murder Case in Georgia Reconstruction, 1868." *Georgia Historical Quarterly* 59:3 (Fall), 296–312.

Davidson, Chandler, and Bernard Grofman. 1994. *Quiet Revolution in the South*. Princeton, NJ: Princeton University Press.

Dawson, Michael. 1994. *Behind the Mule: Race and Class in African-American Politics*. Princeton, NJ: Princeton University Press.

Derfner, Armand. 1984. "Vote Dilution and the Voting Rights Act Amendments of 1982," in Chandler Davidson (ed.), *Minority Vote Dilution*. Washington, DC: Howard University Press.

DeSantis, John. 2016. *The Thibodaux Massacre: Racial Violence and the 1887 Sugar Cane Labor Strike*. Charleston, SC: The History Press.

Devos, Thierry, and Mahzarin R. Banaji. 2005. "American = White?" *Journal of Personality and Social Psychology* 88:3, 447–466.

Dixon, Alan. 2013. *The Gentleman from Illinois: Stories from Forty Years of Elective Public Service*. Carbondale: Southern Illinois University Press.

Doyle, William. 2001. *An American Insurrection: The Battle of Oxford, Mississippi*. New York: Doubleday.

Du Bois, W. E. B. 1935. *Black Reconstruction in America*. New York: Harcourt Brace, and Company.

Dudziak, Mary. 2000. *Cold War Civil Rights: Race and the Image of American Democracy*. Princeton, NJ: Princeton University Press.

Dunning, William. 1907. *Reconstruction, Political and Economic*. New York: Harper, and Brothers.

Farrington, Joshua. 2016. *Black Republicans and the Transformation of the GOP*. Philadelphia: University of Pennsylvania Press.

Fitzgerald, Michael. 1989. *The Union League Movement in the Deep South*. Baton Rouge: Louisiana State University Press.

Fleming, Walter. 1919. *The Sequel at Appomattox*. New Haven, CT: Yale University Press.

Flynt, Wayne. 2004. *Alabama in the Twentieth Century*. Tuscaloosa: University of Alabama Press.

Foner, Eric. 1987. "Rights and the Constitution in Black Life during the Civil War and Reconstruction." *Journal of American History* 74:3, 863–883.

Foner, Eric. 1988. *Reconstruction: America's Unfinished Revolution, 1863–1877*. New York: Harper & Row.

Foner, Eric. 1993. *Freedom's Lawmakers: A Directory of Black Officeholding During Reconstruction*. Oxford: Oxford University Press.

Formwalt, Lee. 1987. "The Camilla Massacre of 1868: Racial Violence as Political Propaganda." *Georgia Historical Quarterly* 71:3 (Fall), 399–426.

Forner, Karlyn. 2017. *Why the Vote Wasn't Enough for Selma*. Durham, NC: Duke University Press.

Fraser, Cary. 2000. "Crossing the Color Line in Little Rock: The Eisenhower Administration and the Dilemma of Race for US Foreign Policy." *Diplomatic History* 24:2, 233–264.

Francis, Megan. 2014. *Civil Rights and the Making of the American State*. Cambridge: Cambridge University Press.

Frielander, Alan, and Richard Gerber. 2019. *Welcoming Ruin: The Civil Rights Act of 1875*. Leiden: Brill.

Frymer, Paul. 2017. *Building an American Empire: The Era of Territorial and Political Expansion*. Princeton, NJ: Princeton University Press.

Frymer, Paul. 1999. *Uneasy Alliances: Race and Party Competition in America*. Princeton, NJ: Princeton University Press.

Garfield, Rachel, Kendal Orgera, and Anthony Damico. 2019. "The Coverage Gap: Uninsured Adults in States that Do Not Expand Medicaid." Kaiser Family Foundation Report, March 21.

Garrow, David. 1978. *Protest at Selma: Martin Luther King, Jr, and the Voting Rights Act of 1965*. New Haven, CT: Yale University Press.

Gatewood, Willard. 1968. "Theodore Roosevelt and the Indianola Affair." *Journal of Negro History* 53:1, 48–69.

Gerstle, Gary. 2015. *Liberty and Coercion*. Princeton, NJ: Princeton University Press.

Gerteis, Joseph. 2003. "Populism, Race, and Political Interest in Virginia." *Social Science History* 27:2, 197–227.

Gibson, Edward, and Desmond King. 2016. "Federalism and Subnational Democratization in the United States," in Jacqueline Behrend, and Laurence Whitehead (eds.), *Illiberal Practices*. Baltimore, MD: Johns Hopkins University Press.

Gillette, William. 1979. *Retreat from Reconstruction*. Baton Rouge: Louisiana State University Press.

Gilmore, Glenda. 2008. *Defying Dixie: The Radical Roots of Civil Rights, 1919–1950*. New York: Norton.

Glausser, Wayne. 1990. "Three Approaches to Locke and the Slave Trade." *Journal of the History of Ideas* 51:2 (Apr–Jun), 199–216.

Gleason, Philip. 1980. "American Identity and Americanization," in William Petersen, Michael Novak, and Philip Gleason (eds.), *Concepts of Ethnicity*. Cambridge, MA: Belknap Press.

Goldin, Claudia. 1974. "The Economics of Emancipation." *Journal of Economic History* 33:1, 66–85.

Gordon, Sarah. 2002. *The Mormon Question: Polygamy and Constitutional Conflict in Nineteenth-Century America*. Chapel Hill: University of North Carolina Press.

Green, Constance. 1967. *The Secret City: A History of Race Relations in the Nation's Capital*. Princeton, NJ: Princeton University Press.

Gutgold, Nichola. 2006. *Paving the Way for Madam President*. Lanham, MD: Lexington Books.

Hackney, Sheldon. 1969. "Southern Violence." *American Historical Review* 74:3, 906–925.

Hamilton, Dona, and Charles Hamilton. 1998. *The Dual Agenda: Race and Social Welfare Policies of Civil Rights Organizations*. New York: Columbia University Press.

Harris, Fred. 2008. *Does People Do It?* Norman: University of Oklahoma Press.

Harris, Fredrick. 2012. *The Price of the Ticket: Barack Obama and the Rise and Decline of Black Politics*. Oxford: Oxford University Press.

Hartz, Louis. 1955. *The Liberal Tradition in America*. New York: Harcourt, Brace, and Company.

Herbert, Hilary. 1901. "The Race Problem at the South." The *Annals of the American Academy of Political and Social Science* 18:1, 95–101.

Hofstadter, Richard. 1955. *The Age of Reform*. New York: Random House.

Hogue, James. 2006. *Uncivil War*. Baton Rouge: Louisiana State University Press.

Horne, Gerald. 2014. *The Counter-Revolution of 1776: Slave Resistance and the Origins of the United States of America*. New York: New York University Press.

Huntington, Samuel. 1981. *American Politics: The Promise of Disharmony*. Cambridge, MA: Harvard University Press.

Hyman, Harold. 1997. *The Reconstruction of Justice Salmon P. Chase*. Lawrence: University Press of Kansas.

Immerwahr, Daniel. 2019. *How to Hide an Empire: A History of the Greater United States*. New York: Farrar, Giroux, and Strauss.

Johnson, Kimberley. 2016. "The Color Line and the State," in Richard Valelly, Suzanne Mettler, and Robert Lieberman (eds.), *The Oxford Handbook of American Political Development*. Oxford: Oxford University Press.

Johnson, Richard. 2017. "Hamilton's Deracialization: Barack Obama's Racial Politics in Context." *Du Bois Review* 14:2 (Fall), 621–628.

Johnson, Richard. 2018. "Proudly for Brooke: Race-Conscious Campaigning in 1960s Massachusetts." *Journal of Race, Ethnicity, and Politics* 3:2 (Sept), 261–292.

Kabaservice, Geoffrey. 2012. *Rule and Ruin.* Oxford: Oxford University Press.

Kaczorowski, Robert. 2005. *The Politics of Judicial Interpretation: The Federal Courts, the Department of Justice, and Civil Rights, 1866–1876.* New York: Fordham University Press.

Kato, Daniel. 2015. *Liberalizing Lynching.* Oxford: Oxford University Press.

Katznelson, Ira. 2013. *Fear Itself: The New Deal and the Origins of Our Time.* New York: Liveright.

Kazin, Michael. 1995. *The Populist Persuasion.* New York: Basic Books.

Kenney, David, and Robert Hartley. 2012 [2003]. *The Heroic and the Notorious: US Senators from Illinois*, 2nd edn. Carbondale: Southern Illinois University Press.

Kilbourne, Richard. 1995. *Debt, Investment, Slaves.* Tuscaloosa: University of Alabama Press.

King, Desmond. 1995. *Separate and Unequal: Black Americans and the US Federal Government.* Oxford: Oxford University Press.

King, Desmond. 2000. *Making Americans: Immigration, Race, and the Origins of Diverse Democracy.* Oxford: Oxford University Press.

King, Desmond. 2017. "Forceful Federalism Against American Racial Inequality." *Government and Opposition* 52:2, 356–382.

King, Desmond, and Robert Lieberman. 2009. "Ironies of State Building: A Comparative Perspective on the American State." *World Politics* 61:3, 547–588.

King, Desmond, and Robert Lieberman. 2019. "The Latter Day General Grant: Federal Power and James Meredith's Desegregation of the University of Mississippi." Paper presented at the annual conference of the American Political Science Association. Washington, DC.

King, Desmond, and Rogers Smith. 2005. "Racial Orders in American Political Development." *American Political Science Review* 99:1, 75–92.

King, Desmond, and Rogers Smith. 2014. "Without Regard to Race? Critical Ideational Developments in Modern American Politics." *Journal of Politics* 76:4, 958–971.

King, Desmond, and Stephen Tuck. 2007. "De-Centering the South: America's Nationwide White Supremacist Order After Reconstruction." *Past & Present* 194:1, 213–253.

Klarman, Michael. 2000. "The Racial Origins of Modern Criminal Procedure." *Michigan Law Review* 99:1 (Oct), 48–97.

Kleintop, Amanda. 2018. "Life, Liberty, and Property in Slaves: White Mississippians Seek 'Just Compensation' for Their Freed Slaves in 1865." *Slavery & Abolition* 39:2, 383–404.

Klingman, Peter. 1976. *Josiah Walls: Florida's First Black Congressman of Reconstruction.* Gainesville: University Press of Florida.

Klinkner, Philip, and Rogers Smith. 1999. *The Unsteady March.* Chicago, IL: University of Chicago Press.

Kousser, J. Morgan. 1984. "The Undermining of the First Reconstruction: Lessons for the Second," in Chandler Davidson (ed.), *Minority Vote Dilution.* Washington, DC: Howard University Press.

Kousser, J. Morgan. 1999. *Colorblind Injustice: Minority Voting Rights and the Undoing of the Second Reconstruction.* Chapel Hill: University of North Carolina Press.

Kousser, J. Morgan. 2015. "Do the Facts of Voting Rights Support Chief Justice Roberts's Opinion in Shelby County." *Transatlantica* 1, 1–31.

Lane, Charles. 2008. *The Day Freedom Died: The Colfax Massacre, the Supreme Court, and the Betrayal of Reconstruction.* New York: Henry Holt.

Lane, Charles. 2019. *Freedom's Detective: The Secret Service, the Ku Klux Klan, and the Man Who Masterminded America's First War on Terror.* Toronto: Hanover Square Press.

Laski, Harold. 1949. *The American Democracy: A Commentary and Interpretation.* London: George Allen and Unwin.

Lebedoff, David. 1969. *The Twenty-First Ballot: A Political Party Struggle in Minnesota.* Minneapolis: University of Minnesota Press.

Lerman, Amy, and Vesla Weaver. 2014. *Arresting Citizenship: The Democratic Consequences of American Crime Control.* Chicago, IL: University of Chicago Press

Levendusky, Matthew. 2009. *The Partisan Sort.* Chicago, IL: University of Chicago Press.

Lippmann, Walter. 1955. *Essays in Public Philosophy.* Boston, MA: Little, Brown, and Company.

Lipset, Seymour Martin. 1950. *Agrarian Socialism: The Cooperative Commonwealth Federation in Saskatchewan*. Berkeley: University of California Press.

Lipset, Seymour Martin. 1963. *The First New Nation: The United States in Historical and Comparative Perspective*. New York: Doubleday.

Longmate, Norman. 1978. *The Hungry Mills: The Story of the Lancashire Cotton Famine, 1861–5*. London: Maurice Temple Smith.

Lubet, Steven. 2010. *Fugitive Justice: Runaways, Rescuers, and Slavery on Trial*. Cambridge, MA: Harvard University Press.

Lublin, David. 1997. *The Paradox of Representation: Racial Gerrymandering and Minority Interests in Congress*. Princeton. NJ: Princeton University Press.

Macpherson, C. B. 1963. *The Political Theory of Possessive Individualism*. Oxford: Oxford University Press.

Maga, Timothy. 1992. "Battling the Ugly American at Home: The Special Protocol Service and the New Frontier, 1961–63." *Diplomacy and Statecraft* 3:1, 126–142.

Malone, Christopher. 2008. *Between Freedom and Bondage: Race, Party, and Voting Rights in the Antebellum North*. New York: Routledge.

Manza, Jeff, and Christopher Uggen. 2006. *Locked Out: Felon Disenfranchisement and American Democracy*. Oxford: Oxford University Press.

Martin, Bonnie. 2010. "Slavery's Invisible Engine: Mortgaging Human Property." *Journal of Southern History* 76:4, 817–866.

Marx, Anthony. 1998. *Making Race and Nation: A Comparison of South Africa, the United States, and Brazil*. Cambridge: Cambridge University Press.

Marx, Karl. 1887 [1867]. *Capital: A Critique of Political Economy*, Volume 1. First English Edition.

May, Gary. 2013. *Bending Toward Justice: The Voting Rights Act and the Transformation of American Democracy*. New York: Basic Books.

Mayer, George. 1964. *The Republican Party, 1854–1964*. Oxford: Oxford University Press.

Mayer, Kenneth R., and Michael G. DeCrescenzo. 2017. *Estimating the Effect of Voter ID on Nonvoters in Wisconsin in the 2016 Presidential Election*. At https://elections.wisc.edu/wp-content/uploads/sites/483/2018/02/Voter-ID-Study-Supporting-Info.pdf.

McConnell, Stuart. 1992. *Glorious Contentment: The Grand Army of the Republic, 1865–1900*. Chapel Hill: University of North Carolina Press.

McCrary, Peyton. 1984. "History in the Courts: The Significance of the *City of Mobile v. Bolden*," in Chandler Davidson (ed.), *Minority Vote Dilution*. Washington, DC: Howard University Press.

McDonald, Laughlin. 1989. "The Quiet Revolution in Voting Rights." *Vanderbilt Law Review* 42, 1249–1298.

McMillan, Malcolm. 1955. *Constitutional Development in Alabama: A Study in Politics, the Negro, and Sectionalism*. Chapel Hill: University of North Carolina Press.

Merritt, Keri Leigh. 2017. *Masterless Men: Poor Whites and Slavery in the Antebellum South*. Cambridge: Cambridge University Press.

Mickey, Robert. 2015. *Paths Out of Dixie: The Democratization of Authoritarian Enclaves in America's Deep South, 1944–1972*. Princeton, NJ: Princeton University Press.

Middleton, Stephen. 2002. *Black Congressmen During Reconstruction: A Documentary Sourcebook*. Westport, CT: Praeger.

Miller, Lisa. 2015. "What's Violence Got to Do with It? Inequality, Punishment, and State Failure in US Politics." *Punishment, and Society* 17:2, 184–210.

Mitau, G. Theodore. 1970 [1960]. *Politics in Minnesota*. Minneapolis: University of Minnesota Press.

Müller, Jan-Werner. 2016. *What is Populism?* Philadelphia: University of Pennsylvania Press.

Muraskin, William. 1975. *Middle-Class Blacks in a White Society: Prince Hall Freemasonry in America*. Berkeley: University of California Press.

Myrdal, Gunnar. 1944. *An American Dilemma*. New York: Harper, and Row.

National Commission on Voting Rights. 2014. *Protecting Minority Voters*. Lawyers' Committee for Civil Rights Under Law.

Newton, Michael. 2010. *The Ku Klux Klan in Mississippi*. Jefferson, NC: McFarland, and Company.

Norris, Pippa, and Ronald Inglehart. 2018. *Cultural Backlash: Trump, Brexit, and the Rise of Authoritarian Populism*. Cambridge: Cambridge University Press.

Novkov, Julie. 2014. "Making Citizens of Freedmen and

Polygamists," in Carol Nackenoff, and Julie Novkov (eds.), *Statebuilding from the Margins: Between Reconstruction and the New Deal*. Philadelphia: University of Pennsylvania Press.

Nixon, Richard. 1957. "The Emergency of Africa: Report to President Eisenhower by Vice-President Nixon." *Department of State Bulletin* 36 (April 22), 635–640.

Orren, Karen, and Stephen Skowronek. 2004. *The Search for American Political Development*. Cambridge: Cambridge University Press.

Oubre, Claude. 1978. *Forty Acres and a Mule: The Freedmen's Bureau and Black Land Ownership*. Baton Rouge: Louisiana State University Press.

Perry, Huey, and Wayne Parent. 1995. "Black Politics in the United States," in Huey L. Perry and Wayne Parent (eds.), *Blacks and the American Political System*. Gainesville: University Press of Florida.

Persily, Nathaniel, Stephen Ansolabehere, and Charles Stewart. 2009. "*Amici Curiae* on Behalf of Neither Party." *NAMUDNO v. Holder*, 129 S. Ct. 2504.

Pettigrew, Thomas, and Denise Alston. 1988. *Tom Bradley's Campaign for Governor: The Dilemma of Race and Political Strategies*. Washington, DC: Joint Center for Political Studies.

Phillips, Kevin. 1969. *The Emerging Republican Majority*. New York: Arlington House.

Polgar, Paul. 2011. "Whenever They Judged It Expedient: The Politics of Partisanship and Free Black Voting Rights in Early New York." *American Nineteenth Century History* 12:1, 1–23.

Reed, Adolph. 2002. "Unraveling the Relation of Race and Class in American Politics," in Diane Davis (ed.), *Political Power and Social Theory*. Bingley: Emerald Group Publishing.

Reed, Adolph. 2002. "The Unravelling of Race and Class in American Politics." *Political Power and Theory* 15, 265–274.

Rhodehamel, John, and Louise Taper (eds.). 1997. *Right or Wrong, God Judge Me: The Writings of John Wilkes Booth*. Urbana: University of Illinois Press.

Richardson, Heather. 2001. *The Death of Reconstruction: Race, Labor, and Politics in the Post-Civil War North, 1865–1901*. Cambridge, MA: Harvard University Press.

Rigueur, Leah Wright. 2015. *The Loneliness of the Black Republican*. Princeton, NJ: Princeton University Press.

Robin, Corey. 2019. *The Enigma of Clarence Thomas.* New York: Metropolitan Books.

Rockwell, Stephen. 2010. *Indian Affairs and the Administrative State in the Nineteenth Century.* Cambridge: Cambridge University Press.

Rogers, William. 1970. *The One-Gallused Rebellion: Agrarianism in Alabama, 1865–1896.* Baton Rouge: Louisiana State University Press.

Rosenberg, Daniel. 1988. *New Orleans Dockworkers: Race, Labor, and Unionism, 1892–1923.* Albany: State University of New York Press.

Rosenthal, Caitlin. 2018. *Accounting for Slavery: Masters and Management.* Cambridge, MA: Harvard University Press.

Sabato, Larry. 1978. *The Democratic Party in Virginia: Tantamount to Election No Longer.* Charlottesville, VA: University of Virginia Press.

Sartre, Jean-Paul. 1943. *L'Être et le néant.* Paris: Bibliothèque des idées.

Saville, Julie. 1996. *The Work of Reconstruction: From Slave to Wage Laborer in South Carolina.* Cambridge: Cambridge University Press.

Sewell, William. 1996. "Historical Events as Transformations of Structures." *Theory and Society* 25:6, 841–881.

Shils, Edward. 1956. *The Torment of Secrecy.* Glencoe, IL: The Free Press.

Shofner, Jerrell. 1973. "Militant Negro Laborers in Reconstruction Florida." *Journal of Southern History* 39 (Aug), 397–408.

Shofner, Jerrell. 1974. *Nor Is It Over Yet: Florida in the Era of Reconstruction, 1863–1877.* Gainesville: University of Florida Press.

Sitkoff, Harvard. 1971. "Harry Truman and the Election of 1948: The Coming of Age of Civil Rights in American Politics." *Journal of Southern History* 37:4 (Nov), 597–616.

Skocpol, Theda. 1992. *Protecting Soldiers and Mothers.* Cambridge, MA: Harvard University Press.

Skocpol, Theda, and Kenneth Finegold. 1982. "State Capacity and Economic Intervention in the Early New Deal." *Political Science Quarterly* 97:2, 255–278.

Sokol, Jason. 2014. *All Eyes Are Upon Us: Race and Politics from Brooklyn to Boston.* New York: Basic Books.

Spero, Sterling, and Abram Harris. 1959. *The Black Worker:*

The Negro and the Labor Movement. New York: Columbia University Press.

Spero, Sterling. 1935. "The Negro's Rule." *Nation* (24 July).

Stanley, Amy Dru. 1998. *From Bondage to Contract: Wage Labor, Marriage, and the Market in the Age of Slave Emancipation*. Cambridge: Cambridge University Press.

Stephenson, D. Grier. 1988. "The Supreme Court, the Franchise, and the Fifteenth Amendment." *University of Missouri Kansas City Law Review* 57, 47–65.

Stewart, David. 2009. *Impeached*. New York: Simon & Schuster.

Tate, Katherine. 1994. *From Protest to Politics: The New Black Voters in American Elections*. Cambridge, MA: Harvard University Press.

Tate, Katherine. 2003. *Black Faces in the Mirror: African Americans and their Representatives in Congress*. Princeton, NJ: Princeton University Press.

Taylor, Keeanga-Yamahtta. 2008. Review: W. E. B. Du Bois: *Black Reconstruction in America, 1860–1880*. *International Socialist Review* 57 (Jan/Feb).

Thorne, Christopher. 1974. "Britain and the Black GIs: Racial Issues and Anglo-American Relations in 1942." *Journal of Ethnic and Migration Studies* 3, 262–271.

Thurber, Timothy. 2013. *Republicans and Race: The GOP's Frayed Relationship with African Americans, 1945–1974*. Lawrence: University Press of Kansas.

Tushnet, Mark. 1999. *Taking the Constitution Away from the Courts*. Princeton, NJ: Princeton University Press.

Uggen, Christopher, and Jeff Manza. 2002. "Democratic Contraction? Political Consequences of Felon Disenfranchisement in the United States." *American Sociological Review* 67:6, 777–803.

Uggen, Christopher, Ryan Larson, and Sarah Shannon. 2016. *Six Million Lost Voters*. Washington, DC: The Sentencing Project.

US Department of Agriculture. 1933. *History of the Southern United States to 1860*, vol. 2. Washington, DC: US Department of Agriculture.

Valelly, Richard. 1989. *Radicalism in the States: The Minnesota Farmer-Labor Party and the American Political Economy*. Chicago, IL: University of Chicago Press.

Valelly, Richard. 2004. *The Two Reconstructions*. Chicago, IL: University of Chicago Press.

Valelly, Richard. 2016. "How Suffrage Politics Made, and Makes, America," in Richard Valelly, Suzanne Mettler, and Robert Lieberman (eds.), *The Oxford Handbook of American Political Development*. Oxford: Oxford University Press.

Van Cleve, George. 2010. *A Slaveholders' Union: Slavery, Politics, and the Constitution in the Early American Republic*. Chicago, IL: University of Chicago Press.

Wade, Wyn. 1998. *The Fiery Cross: The Klu Klux Klan in America*. Oxford: Oxford University Press.

White, G. Edward. 1993. "Reconstructing the Constitutional Jurisprudence of Salmon P. Chase." *Northern Kentucky Law Review* 21, 41–116.

White, Richard. 2017. *The Republic for Which It Stands*. Oxford: Oxford University Press.

White, Ronald. 2016. *American Ulysses: A Life of Ulysses S Grant*. New York: Random House.

Whitfield, Stephen. 1988. *A Death in the Delta*. Baltimore, MD: Johns Hopkins University Press.

Witt, Andrew. 2007. *The Black Panthers and the Midwest*. New York: Routledge.

Wolf, Martin. 2017. "The Economic Origins of the Populist Surge," *Financial Times*, June 27.

Wolters, Raymond. 1996. *Right Turn: William Bradford Reynolds, the Reagan Administration, and Black Civil Rights*. New Brunswick, NJ: Transaction Publishers.

Woodward, C. Vann. 1951. *Origins of the New South, 1877-1913*. Baton Rouge: Louisiana State University Press.

Woodward, C. Vann. 1957. "The Political Legacy of Reconstruction." *Journal of Negro Education* 26:3 (Summer), 231–240.

Woodward, C. Vann. 1966. *The Strange Career of Jim Crow*, 2nd rev. edn. Oxford: Oxford University Press.

Zackin, Emily. 2013. *Looking for Rights in All the Wrong Places*. Princeton, NJ: Princeton University Press.

Index

Index